AN HISTORICAL ACCOUNT OF THE SETTLEMENT AND POSSESSION OF BOMBAY

AN HISTORICAL ACCOUNT OF THE SETTLEMENT AND POSSESSION OF BOMBAY

BY THE ENGLISH EAST INDIA COMPANY, AND OF THE RISE AND PROGRESS OF THE WAR WITH THE MAHRATTA NATION

PECHEL SAMUEL

GYAN

Published by

Gyan Publishing House
5, Ansari Road
Daryaganj, New Delhi-110002
Phone: 011-47034999, 9811692060
E-mail: books@gyanbooks.com

Distribution Network
gyanbooks.com
India, USA, Canada, UK, Australia

ISBN: 978-93-7133-091-6 (PB)

First Published, 1781

2nd Impression 2025

Printed at: Gyan Press, Delhi.

AN HISTORICAL ACCOUNT OF THE SETTLEMENT AND POSSESSION OF BOMBAY

Author: PECHEL SAMUEL

AN HISTORICAL ACCOUNT OF THE SETTLEMENT AND POSSESSION OF BOMBAY, BY THE ENGLISH EAST INDIA COMPANY, AND OF THE RISE AND PROGRESS OF THE WAR WITH THE MAHRATTA NATION.

LONDON:

Printed by W. Richardson, Strand,
For J. ROBSON, Bookfeller, New Bond-ftreet.

M.DCCLXXXI.

ADVERTISEMENT.

THE following narrative was not begun with a view to publication; it hath been continued to the beginning of the last year at the desire of some respectable persons. Mr. Orme's *history, and that of the decline of the Mogul empire by* Mr. Dow, *together with the relations of the most credible travellers, have furnished some of the materials; the records of the India Company the remainder.—Truth and impartiality have been the writer's aim—the reader will judge whether he hath succeeded.*

E R R A T A.

Page 9, l. 13, *for* even *read* ever.
30, 1, *for* Cattack *r.* Cuttack.
43, 7, *for* which *r.* this.
45, 24, *for* Furrat *r.* Amrut.
55, 16, *for* Peut *r.* Pont.
64, 20, *read* Morabah, Butchabah, and Bobagee Naig,
76, ult. *for* Uguie *r.* Uguien.
104, 17, *after* ruined *place a* Comma.
122, 2, *for* Mahi *r.* Mahé.
140, 17, *for* , *place* full Stop *and for* that *r.* That.
142, 6, *for* have *r.* had—l. 11, *for* is *r.* was.
149, 22, *r.* their minifter. *Laſt word r.* therefore.
158, ult. *r.* Mangalore.
228, 6, *dele* to.
267, 9, *r.* of which.
277, 20, *for* Carnac *r.* Camac.
294, 8, *r.* he was.
308, 5, *for* Myhic *r.* Myhie.
310, 9, *after* property *place a* Comma.
319, 12, *after* Owde *place a* Comma.
335, 15, *for* had *r.* hath.

AN

ACCOUNT

OF THE

SETTLEMENT AND POSSESSION

OF

BOMBAY, &c.

THE iſland of Bombay is the antient property of the Engliſh Eaſt India Company; it hath hitherto been, of all her ſettlements, the moſt conducive to the greatneſs of the nation in Aſia; yet, through the ſplendor of atchievement, great acquiſition of territory, and immenſe harveſts of wealth in Bengal and the Coaſt of Coromandel, it hath been in ſome meaſure overlooked, and, as if in a corner of the world, unnoticed.

It receives great importance as well from its ſituation, ſo advantageous not only in regard to external trade and the internal in

the

the neighbouring provinces, as from the docks which are the only ones the Company have in India, and without which therefore there can be no maritime power in thoſe regions. Hitherto the expence of maintaining hath not been defrayed by the produce; but the preſent ſituation of affairs in the neighbouring provinces, well improved, may place things on a different foot, and that expence not only be cleared, but a conſiderable revenue yielded, and a great influence in the weſtern part of Indoſtan obtained. Some account therefore of this ſettlement, and of the events which have offered this occaſion of ſo favourable a change, may be uſeful at this time.

In the midway between Goa and Surat on the Malabar Coaſt, the land from Baſſein to Choul bends into a deep bay, in which lie the iſlands of Salcet, Bombay, Caranjah, Hog Iſland, Elephanta, and Canary. Salcet is the moſt northern, ſeparated from the continent by ſo ſmall a channel that it is called a river: on the Eaſt the diſtance is greater, but the channel is fordable. It is about twenty miles long and as many broad. Its waters are wholeſome; its ſoil fruitful, naturally abundant, and capable of great improvement;

provement; the produce is moſtly rice; it was formerly the granary of Goa. Half a mile to the South of this lies the iſland of Bombay, about eight miles long and twenty in circumference. Its diſtance from the continent is about eight miles, and its ſituation forms the harbour. It is well peopled, notwithſtanding the water is bad. Caranjah produces rice to the value of 60,000 roupies a year; Elephanta, of about 8,000; the others are little better than rocks.

In the year 1661, the Portugueze being then maſters of that bay and thoſe iſlands, they were given to Charles the Second as part of his Queen's dowry. But the people ſettled there did not eaſily yield poſſeſſion; for, when a fleet of five ſhips, with five hundred land forces, was ſent by the King of England, with the proper muniments from the court of Liſbon, entrance was refuſed. This expedition was commanded by Lord Mallborough, who, on this refuſal, carried the fleet to Swally, which lies to the North of Surat: the jealouſy of the inhabitants obliged them to retire; the only place open to them was

* A roupie is worth, when remitted to England, from 2 s. to 2 s. 3 d.

Angediva, an uninhabited iſland to the ſouthward of Goa. Lord Mallborough left them there, and returned ſingly to Bombay, where, after much altercation, he prevailed to be admitted, firſt to the town, and afterwards to the poſſeſſion of the whole iſland and the bay. But during his abſence the unhealthineſs of the climate, ſeconded by intemperance, had made havock among the unfortunate perſons who had been carried to Angediva; three hundred of them had periſhed; the few who remained were admitted in the year 1664. Their firſt care was to make the iſland defendable. The Portugueze corrupted by eaſe and luxury had ſunk in indolence, and were regardleſs of every thing, but what contributed to their pleaſure: gardens adorned their poſſeſſions, but fortifications were totally neglected. Mr. Cook, who commanded that diminiſhed force, was the firſt governor; he was immediately under the crown; but this government was not of long continuance: for the King finding no advantage to himſelf from that poſſeſſion, but on the contrary being put to great expence in ſending out ſhips, wiſhed to be rid of it. The officers and men ſent in thoſe ſhips drove a private trade, which impaired that

that of the Company; and their licentiousness often engaged them in hostilities with the natives, for which the Company was answerable to the powers of that country. These real evils, and the advantage to be reaped from the possession of that island and bay, made the Company desire it; they therefore requested, and the King readily granted them: from that time they have had the absolute dominion.

The island was at first governed by deputies from the English factory at Surat. Dissention soon arose between the civil and military power, and grew to such a height, that in the year 1671 all was confusion. To put an end to this, and to fortify the island against attempts, which he foresaw a probability of, from the Dutch, then at war with England, Mr. Aungier, president of the factory of Surat, being also disgusted by the arrogance of the Mogul governor of that town, changed his residence and established himself at Bombay, where his prudence quashed the dissentions, his good management advanced the Company's interest, and his activity secured the island: insomuch, that in the spring of

 1672,

1672, the Dutch attempting a ſurprize, found the fort ſo well guarded, and every thing in ſo good a condition, that they immediately gave over the enterprize.

From that period, each day ſhewing the great importance of this ſettlement, the reſidence of the governor was fixed there, and the ſeveral factories on the Coaſt of Malabar, and in the Perſian Gulph, became dependent on that preſidency.

Notwithſtanding the natural inconveniences of this iſland in the want of ſprings and ſtreams of freſh water, and the poorneſs of its natural produce, from the time of the poſſeſſion of the Engliſh, its populouſneſs became conſiderable. Many were invited by the freedom granted to all religions, and the mildneſs of the government; (that of the Engliſh, even when puſhed to what would ſeem tyranny at home, appearing gentle to thoſe who had felt Mahometan inſolence and Portugueze bigotry) inſomuch, that from ten thouſand ſouls, the utmoſt of its inhabitants when in poſſeſſion of theſe, they were in the year 1764 augmented to ſixty thouſand.

The

The acceſs to the harbour and its ſafety in all ſeaſons, with its vicinity to the country inhabited by the Maharattas, and the conveniency of a paſs over the Gaut * Mountains, through which the inland parts may be ſupplied with our merchandize, are great advantages, the ſale of woollen and other Engliſh goods there, amounting annually to fourteen lacks of roupies †. The convenience of the harbour hath produced a trade of Indian commodities with that country, almoſt excluſive; as alſo a very conſiderable one in the cotton, with which Bengal is ſupplied, whereby the cuſtoms bring the Company an annual profit of three lacks and a half ‡. The proximity of Surat gives an influence in that government, which, if rightly exerted, may prove of immenſe benefit; as Surat is, next to Bombay, the great mart for our ſtaple commodities. Through theſe advantages the trade may fall almoſt totally into the hands of the Engliſh.

What is yet of greater conſequence, not only to the Company but the nation, is the

* Gaut or Gatte means paſſage.

† 140,000 l. at 2 s. per roupie.

‡ 35,000 l. at 2 s. the common exchange is 2 s. 3 d.

maritime power which arises from this possession. Docks are constructed there sufficient not only for repairing, but building of ships. To these it is easy to bring excellent timber * from the continent, particularly from Bassein; a number of artificers are settled there, so that every repair and building may be done as perfectly as in England. This convenience is not to be found in any other part of that, or the Coromandel Coast, nor even in Bengal; and to this resource may in a great measure be attributed the success of England in that region during the last war. But the great expence attending this settlement hath hitherto counterbalanced these advantages; the profits arising from the territory, and the great trade carried on, not being equal to the amount of that expence. This hath made some further advantage in these parts necessary, and this necessity hath been most strongly felt since the year 1768, when there were great additions made to the fortifications, and the military establishment was augmented; a wise measure! so necessary that it is to be

* The Teke tree, called by Fryer the Indian oak, grows in all those parts. It is better from its durability in water than our oak. Ships built of that wood, and used in the country trade, last twenty or thirty years, and longer.

wondered

wondered that no inconvenience aroſe during the long time it remained neglected.

By the great ſums then expended, and the laſting increaſe of that eſtabliſhment, the defect before-mentioned became grievous, and moſtly when it was neceſſary to furniſh inveſtments for Europe and China. The only remedy was the acquiſition of a territory ſufficient by its revenues to defray the expence of the eſtabliſhment. The iſland of Salcet, Baſſein, and its territory, immediately preſented themſelves as the proper objects for this purpoſe, when even an opportunity ſhould offer to acquire them from the Maharattas who were then the poſſeſſors of them. The ſituation and nature of Salcet have been already deſcribed; its produce is ſuch that it almoſt ſuffices for the ſupply of Bombay, which, with the aid of Caranjah and Baſſein may, however numerous its people, be ſecure of proviſion of every kind. Baſſein is neceſſary to the proviſion of timber wanted for the Company's docks, which, ſhould it fall in the hands of an enemy, or a quarrel ariſe with its poſſeſſors, might become uſeleſs for want of materials. The importance of thoſe objects, ſo much greater than that of the ſupply

ſupply of expence, hath ſo ſtrongly ſtruck the Directors, that they have repeatedly and urgently enjoined that preſidency to ſeize every opportunity of acquiring theſe poſſeſſions, and to that principally to direct their views and operations: but as the poſſeſſors are equally ſenſible of thoſe advantages, and conſequently of the value of their poſſeſſion, there was little proſpect of ſucceſs, when, in the year 1773, the diſorders which diſturbed the government of the Maharatta ſtate afforded the occaſion ſo much wiſhed. That theſe events may be underſtood, it is neceſſary to give ſome account of the people among whom they happened: a people who have hitherto had no regular place in hiſtory; mentioned only curſorily as freebooters or barbarians, although ſettled in a regular government, and the moſt conſiderable nation in India; whether we regard the extent of their territory, their ſituation, or their arms.

The rapidity of ſucceſs which ſo wonderfully extended the empire of the Mahometans, attended thoſe who invaded India. The princes of that immenſe region were in general overwhelmed: divided among themſelves they aſſiſted their conquerors; yet many

many of them, whilſt they yielded, preſerved their dominions by paying a tribute, and acknowledging the ſovereignty of the victors; and others refuſing this, by arms kept up their independence. They, whoſe poſſeſſions lay in the low, plain, and fertile part of the country, being leſs able to reſiſt, were in the firſt claſs; but they who dwelt among the mountains, hardy and uſed to arms, and protected by the roughneſs of their ſituation, were not to be eaſily ſubdued. They not only reſiſted, but often baffled the power of the mightieſt emperors: even Aurengzebe found it neceſſary to prefer art to force; and, by being ſatisfied with ſmall acknowledgments, prevailed by cunning where his arms muſt have failed. The kingdom of Viſiapour was thus at laſt ſubdued by him; and the king brought to his court, remained there maintained by a penſion as one of his Omrahs; but a part of that kingdom inhabited by a hardy race, who before that revolution had thrown off the ſubjection to the king, remained unconquered; and continued not only free from the yoke of the Moguls, but at laſt ſaw that empire tributary to them.

These

These tribes extended from the territory of Surat to that of Goa along the sea coast, and backward over the mountains to the city of Visiapour, and are at this day known by the name of Maharattas. The history of the Hindoos gives them great antiquity, even to the most remote times *. They have preserved their original manners and religion; scrupulous observers of that of Bramah, they never feed on any thing which hath had animal life; temperate, sober, indefatigable; always in arms; inured to all hardships, capable of resisting heat and climate. A numerous cavalry mounted on horses as hardy in their nature as their riders, is the strength of their army: their marches are incredibly long and rapid: they avoid general engagements; retreating with a celerity as sudden as that with which they invaded, they mark the country they leave with the misery of plunder and devastation; they return as soon as the army raised by the prince, whose territory they invade, hath been disbanded. Thus all the horrors of this predatory war are renewed, to the total destruction of the wretched inhabitants. Hence the difficulty of reaching

* Orme. Dow.

them,

them, and the detriment arising from these inroads induce the princes of the invaded countries to purchase their retreat, either by a large contribution, or stipulating to pay an annual tribute. Their arms have extended this kind of conquest even to the gates of Dehli. Expences in luxury are unknown to them; and continually collecting from the countries they pass over, immense treasures are brought to remain in theirs; which, whilst the provinces within their reach have been ravaged and exhausted, have continued in undisturbed tranquillity. The policy of the original constitution of their government forbad the extension of their territorial dominions. This law, notwithstanding the success attending their arms, and the incitements of ambition common to conquerors, continued long inviolate, their views leading them no further than the imposition of a tribute they called Chout, one fourth of the estimated clear revenue of the countries they subdued: this, in a course of time, became general through the greatest part of India. Their resources of wealth were simple, and unembarrassed by territorial arrangements; their armies numerous in proportion to their immense revenues, and their country easy of defence.

defence. But by degrees the ambitious and interested views of powerful individuals brought them to depart from this policy, and to extend their territorial possessions. From that time their government no longer retained a consistent system of measures, but became a disjointed union of different interests and dependencies, where each chief, accommodating the interests of the state to what suited his, acted solely for his own purpose.

The revolution by which these tribes became an independent nation *, was owing to a bold Raypout of the kingdom of Visiapour, named Seva or Sava †, who had long dwelt in the mountains, where he was at the head of a bold set of adventurers. This man was descended from an ancient line of Rajas, of the cast of the Bouncelos, a warlike and active race. His grandfather, Vanga Gi, was high in office under Nizam Shaw the last prince of Guzurat; and by him was Seva's father, Shaw Gi Raja, made commander of Jenneah Gur, where Seva was born, as was also a second son called Samba; by another

* Fryer.

† He is commonly called Seva Gi. This additional syllable denotes some rank or honour; as chief.

wife

wiſe he had a third ſon named Ekou. When Nizam Shaw was ſubdued by Aurengzebe, Shaw Gi, and his two younger ſons, entered into the ſervice of the king of Viſiapour, where they were raiſed to great employments; the father to the command of the king's guard, Samba to a jaguier of ten thouſand horſe, and twenty thouſand foot, with thirty lacks of roupies a year, and Ekou to one of two thouſand horſe and eight thouſand foot, with ten lacks of roupies a year. Seva would not ſubmit to ſerve any prince, but, gathering a party, maintained himſelf and them by inroads upon the plain country; ſometimes againſt the ſubjects of the Mogul, at others againſt thoſe of Viſiapour. Nor could he ever be brought by the inſtances of his father and his brothers to change this courſe of life, which diſobedience occaſioned ſo heavy a reſentment from his father, that he excluded him from his ſucceſſion. The king of Viſiapour, upon ſome ſuſpicions of machinations againſt him, put to death Shaw Gi Rajah: revenge of this murder furniſhed Seva an excuſe for puſhing on his devaſtations. The king ſent a ſtrong army againſt him, under the command of Abdul Cawn; Seva, finding it much ſuperior

to

to any he could raiſe, whilſt it was yet at a great diſtance, pretended that he was deſirous of yielding obedience, and requeſted his advancing with a ſmall party to a choultry which ſtood between the two armies, that he might there kiſs his feet, and pray him to ſolicit his pardon from the king. Abdul too eaſily believed him, and advancing with his ſon, and an inconſiderable retinue, came to the place appointed. Seva waited there for him, accompanied by few; but he had placed a ſtrong party in ambuſh, who lay totally concealed. He, ſeemingly unarmed, advancing proſtrated himſelf at Abdul's feet, and with tears requeſted his interceſſion with the king. As they entered the choultry Seva ſaid, "You, my lord, may execute your pleaſure on me, and eaſe me of my life." Upon which Abdul, that his fears might vaniſh, and to ſhew him an entire confidence, gave his ſword and poynard to his page. They then begun their conference, when Seva drew a ſtilletto from his ſleeve, and ſtabbed him to the heart. Abdul the ſon flew on Seva and wounded him; but the men in ambuſh ruſhed into the choultry at that moment, a ſcuffle enſued, in which, fortunately Abdul eſcaped; and by putting on a mean dreſs; and, flying through unfrequented ways, reached his camp; where the tragical end of their general was no ſooner known, than all the troops diſperſed.

Seva, that he might not loſe the fruit of his crime, immediately marched to Panala, a wealthy and ſtrong city, hoping to ſurprize it; but the citizens were on their guard. He, therefore fearing that a ſiege would be long, and give time for another army to be ſent againſt him, which in the plain and open country he could not cope with, endeavoured a ſtratagem. Seven hundred of his followers were employed for this purpoſe. To many of their officers he publicly gave ill-uſage; they loudly complained; and, ſeeming from reſentment his bitter enemies, departed to the town, and offered their ſervice againſt him. They were well received; and though at firſt the inhabitants uſed caution, yet in a very ſhort time their indolence and luxury drawing them to confidence in theſe new friends, they left the guard of the walls moſtly to them: as they had ſought pleaſure more than ſecurity, the ramparts and outworks were pleaſing walks ſhadowed with trees; under the cover of theſe a detachment of Seva's army approached undiſcovered, and were the ſucceeding night admitted by their friends. The inhabitants were ſoon overpowered, and at Seva's mercy, who conſidered them as his ſubjects, and made their city his retreat; adding to the fortifications, and deſtroying the trees which had rendered the former uſeleſs: from this place he over-ran the adjacent country. The king ſoon ſent a freſh force againſt him, under the command of Abdul; this conſiſted of the troops lately diſperſed, and a body of cavalry under Ruſtan Gemma, who had a jaguire of thirty lacks of roupies a year, for which he maintained ten thouſand horſe and thirty thouſand foot; but Seva found means to gain him. Abdul advanced gallantly, and with a ſmall band of choſen friends ruſhed to that part where Seva was, calling him aloud to an encounter; but Seva, who depended upon more than valour, deſpiſed the challenge, anſwering, "The raſh "youth may fall by other hands." In the mean time Ruſtan's horſe diſbanded, and he, with a ſmall party, went over to Seva: Abdul with his few brave friends broke through and reached Viſiapour, his whole army diſperſing, left Seva maſter of the field. Ruſtan adviſed advifed Seva to take advantage of the prefent confternation, and march directly to Vifiapour; he followed his counfel, and his boldnefs would have fucceeded, had not Siddy Jore another jaghedar advanced to the relief of the city, with a body fo confiderable, his own troops being increafed by the re-affemblage of the difperfed army, that Seva could not ftand before it, but was obliged to retreat to Panala. Siddy encamped near the town; Seva, whofe ftratagems never failed him, contrived to efcape, and proceeded to Rajapour, the chief city and fortrefs of Siddy, where he produced a forged phirmaund *, fealed with Siddy's feal, whereby it was fignified, that having exchanged this fortrefs for Panala, the commander was ordered to deliver it up to Seva. Siddy, not able to do any thing againft Panala, returned to Vifiapour. The king fufpected him of treachery, yet received him with a fair countenance, and made him the ufual prefents upon his difmiffion; but, foon after changing his mind, gave orders to Bullul Cawn, whom he made commander in chief, to overtake and deftroy him. Siddy, when Bullul reached him, encountered and defeated him. The king then marched

* A grant.

in perſon againſt him, having by ſecret means gained ſeveral of Siddy's army, who, not miſtruſting the treaſon, joined battle, in which, being forſaken, he was ſlain. This treatment of Siddy Jore incited Siddy Maſſuie, another potent jaghedar, to vengeance; and thus civil diſcord completed the miſery of this kingdom. In the mean time Seva, improving the opportunity, ſecured ſeveral ſmall places towards the ſea coaſt. In the midſt of this confuſion the king died without iſſue; upon his death his widow aſcended the throne; and, by the weakneſs of her government, furniſhed Seva further occaſion of gratifying his revenge, and indulging his ambition. The queen had, during the life of her huſband, conceived a parental fondneſs for a youth named Sikendar, whom ſhe had educated in the doctrine of Ali, the ſect of Mahometans which prevailed in Perſia. She now adopted him, and gave him the title of king: this could not fail of being odious to a people of all others the moſt ſcrupulouſly attached to their religion. Seva was highly eſteemed for his valour, and either from principle or political views, a ſtrict profeſſor of the Gentoo religion, had acquired a great intereſt among the Bramins. Improving theſe advantages, he extended his influence

influence among the Raypouts. The ſcruples of many, and the diſcontents of more, increaſed his company of adventurers to an army, at the head of which he unexpectedly appeared. The queen was totally unprepared. Each advantage improving his force, he reduced into his poſſeſſion the fortreſſes of Rajapur, Raſejeir, and a great part of the Malabar Coaſt; in Raſejeir he was ſaid to have found great treaſures. His ſucceſs was ſuch, that the queen, in the year 1674, before her adopted ſon Sikendar could attain his majority, was obliged to enter into a treaty with him. By the peace which followed, he obtained the independent dominion of the territory and forts which he had conquered.

Unfortunately for the queen and Sikendar this diminution was followed by a worſe. Pammaich, another of the Raypouts tributary to her, truſting to the inacceſſible mountains which ſurrounded his country, revolted, and was ſucceſsful; his faſtneſſes for a long time protecting him.

Her principal forces being employed in the reduction of this rebel, Aurengzebe ſeized this opportunity, and marching to the city of Visiapour, conquered that and the fortress after a three years resistance; the unhappy Sikendar was taken prisoner. Aurengzebe carried him to his court, where he resided as one of his omrahs, enjoying a pension of a million of roupies. This revolution happened in the year 1685.

From the time Seva found himself established by this peace, he assumed the title of Raja Seva Gi, and a regal state, had a pompous coronation, and applied himself closely to make his conquest a valuable dominion: he fortified the principal passes in the mountains, and placed therein faithful lieutenants and good garrisons. His conquests extended to the territory of Surat northward, and southward to that of Goa: the coast between these two places became a part of his possession. This enabled him not only to harrass the country round him by continual incursions, but also to stop all commerce, both of the Portugueze and the subjects of the emperor, by his depredations, insomuch that each of these powers were happy to receive his terms. The possession of so considerable a tract of sea coast inspired him with the idea of of acquiring a maritime power; his late succefs in his depredations gave probability to the fcheme; and his activity in the purfuit of it was fuch, that in a fhort time his force was fufficient, not only to refift, but even to beat a fleet the Mogul emperor had equipped againft him. Thus both at fea and land was his dominion eftablifhed.

In the year 1674, the prefidency of Bombay fent an embaffy to him to treat concerning a trade to be carried on through his country; in which negotiation they afked the fame privileges they enjoyed in Perfia and Indoftan. This was a favourable time for them, as their gallant behaviour, in repulfing an attack he had made upon Surat, had impreffed him with an idea of their valour: he therefore willingly granted them leave to come to Raree, a ftrong hold in the Gatte *, where he then refided. They proceeded from Upper Choul, a confiderable fea-port in his poffeffion, and, after many difficulties, came the fourth day to Puuchara, a town at the foot of the mountain on which Raree ftands: there they pitched their tents, and waited for

* Gatte fignifies a pafs.

his return from a pilgrimage he made to a famous pagoda called Purtabgur, preparatory to his coronation, which they were ſpectators of, and of his fourth marriage. Theſe were to him ſuch ſerious matters, that, till all the ceremonies of faſting and purification were over (during which he and his family were ſhut up with the bramins) the ambaſſadors could not treat of buſineſs with him perſonally, but were referred to Moro Pundit his Paſhwa, or chancellor, who was to report to him the demands they made: their preſents were accepted, and their reception was courteous. Sava Gi owed his ſucceſs in a great meaſure to the influence of the bramins; an incident, trifling in itſelf, ſhews his attention to keep well with their tribe, during this time of his receſs he was weighed in gold, and 16,000 pagodas found to be his weight, were, with 100,000 more, diſtributed among the bramins on the day of his coronation *.

Except

* The great influence of the bramins over the people gave infinite advantage to thoſe whoſe cauſe they eſpouſed. They were revered by the higheſt. In the hiſtory of Ferishta, tranſlated by Dow, page 4. vol. I. anno 977. "It was then cuſtomary among the Rajas, in affairs of "moment, to aſſemble the Double Council, which con-"ſiſted of an equal number of the moſt reſpectable bra-"mins

Except making the English coin current in his dominions, and restoring wrecks of ships perished on his coasts, the whole that was demanded was granted, with this compliment, that with great satisfaction he embraced our friendship, promising to himself and his country much happiness by our settlement and trade.

Seva's success gained him not only territory but dependents. Many of the Rayputs, who were tributaries to the Mogul and king of Visiapour, wearied by the state of war in which they were obliged to live, and seeing an advantage in being under his protection, as they would for a smaller tribute paid to him, not only save their land from devastation, but share the benefit of his manner of maintaining himself (the spoils of the neighbouring countries) became his jaghedars or feudatories; paying him an annual sum, and stipulating to furnish a certain number of troops whenever occasion required:

" mins, who sat on the right of the throne, and of the " nobles, Keitrees, who sat on the left;" but they seem only to be advisers; for there the Raja, to his ruin, against the unanimous opinion of such a council, continued a war against the emperor of Ghizni.

quired:

quired: and thus was formed that federal union which constitutes the Maharatta state. Each of these jaghedars maintains a certain number of troops, with which, when they are not engaged in the common cause, they make incursions in the neighbouring provinces; Sometimes settling in those parts which lie most conveniently for their purpose; at others, being satisfied with the chout or tribute. As the princes from whom this tribute is exacted are impatient of this yoke, to which they yield only through necessity, the Mahometans, who look on themselves as the conquerors of India, feeling deeply the indignity of submitting to persons whom they look on merely as freebooters, whenever they find an opportuity of evading these payments, either from any addition to their strength, or embarrassments among the Maharattas, with-hold them, which the others, as soon as they find it feasible, fail not to demand with an armed force; and thus their troops are kept up, and their inclination to plunder gratified.

The dissentions and war among the successors of Aurengzebe left those of Seva at liberty to strengthen and establish themselves: the

the luxury of the prince, and infidelity of the chief omrahs, dissolved the government of the Mogul empire. In the interval of time passed from the year 1707 *, in which Aurengzebe died, to the year 1718, when Mahommed Shaw ascended the throne, four princes reigned, three of whom were exalted, and then were deprived of life by the faction of the Seids, Abdalla Cawn, and Hassen Cawn. Mahommed, soon after his accession, rid himself of these tyrants, and then sunk in indolence and the pleasures of his haram; the omrahs were at liberty to form and execute schemes of independence in their governments. The most considerable among these, for extent of province and number of troops, were the Nizam ul Mulluck who commanded in the Decan, and Aliverdy Cawn who commanded in Bengal. This omrah by his arms subdued the Rajas who were his neighbours, but tamely permitted the Maharattas to range through the interior parts of the empire. These invasions were so successful in the kingdom of Malava and the neighbouring provinces, that Mahommed, to purchase their retreat, consented to pay them

* Dow's History of the Decline of the Mogul Empire.

the

the chout, or fourth part of the revenues of thoſe provinces. Thus did the ſucceſſor of Tamerlane, and great-grandſon of Aurengzebe, become their tributary.

The whole province of Guzurat, and country as far as the Indus, was in this manner ſubjected to them, and a part of it in the actual poſſeſſion of ſome of their chiefs or jaghedars.

The invaſion of the Perſian Nadir, through the treachery of the Nizam, having exhauſted the provinces, occaſioned the tribute to run in arrear; this furniſhed the pretence, as the weakneſs of the empire did the opportunity, of another invaſion. An army of eighty thouſand horſe under the command of Rago Gi, in 1740, invaded the Carnatic; having forced the paſſes of the mountains, they ſurprized and defeated the army of Doaſt Aly the nabob of the province, who with his ſon fell in the action. Sipander the ſon, and Chunda a Saib, the ſon-in-law of Doaſt Ali, were at variance, and, inſtead of uniting to repel this invaſion, ſhut themſelves up, the firſt in Vellour, the latter in Tritchinopoli. Thus left maſters of the province they ravaged it, it, and raiſed heavy contributions. Sipander ſet on foot a negotiation, which ended in a ſtipulation to pay them a hundred lacks of roupies, and put them in poſſeſſion of the territory of Tritchinopoly. Sipander was acknowledged Nabob. They then retired; but ſix months after returned to take poſſeſſion of the land yielded to them. Chunda Saib ſuſtained a three months ſiege in Tritchinopoly, and then was obliged to ſurrender at diſcretion. Madhar Row, who commanded there in the year 1741, ſold it for a ſum of money to Abdulla Cawn, one of the Nizam generals.

In this year they demanded the chout from the emperor, who, unable to pay it, gave them a commiſſion to gather it in the provinces of Bengal, Bahar, and Oriſſa, where Aliverdi had made himſelf independent. The Suu Raja ſent an army of 50,000 horſe from Sattarah, his capital, to invade Bengal, under the conduct of Boſcar Pundit; they ravaged all the diſtricts weſt of the Ganges. Aliverdi reſiſted them by arms and intrigue: he found means to have their leader aſſaſſinated; the army retreated: but the Raja ſent two other armies, one by the way of Bahar, commanded by Balla Row. and another

another by Cattack, under the command of Rago Gi. Aliverdi contrived to ſow diſſention between theſe chiefs, and treated ſeparately with Balla Row, who having received two years chout evacuated the province. Rago Gi retreated to Cattack, whence with flying parties he harraſſed the provinces: in ſome time Aliverdi prevailed upon him to return likewiſe.

In the year 1750 they retreated from the ſouthern provinces of the empire, in purſuance of an alliance with Ahmed the ſon of Mohammed, who was then defending himſelf againſt the Patans. By this treaty it was ſtipulated, that the chout ſhould be regularly paid. The confuſion which reigned in Dehli prevented this, and furniſhed an occaſion of continual incurſions, which the wars, harraſſing the ſouthern provinces, made ever ſucceſsful. This proſperous ſtate continued till their diſtractions at home engaged their whole attention.

Seva Gi, in modelling his riſing empire, followed the genius of the Gentoo ſyſtem; among them, the Raja has the ſupreme authority, is maſter of peace and war, and abſolutely

ſolutely commands the armies; but, by uſage coeval with their law, is bound, from the moſt learned among the bramins, to form a council, which aſſiſts him in the adminiſtration of juſtice, both in regard to puniſhments and the deciſion of property: their authority is ſimilar to that which Cæſar attributes to the Druids in Britain. Thus the human law, being ſupported by the divine, muſt have found perfect obedience in a nation ſo bigotted to the tenets of their religion; the firſt of which is, that the bramins are of a race ſuperior to other mortals, who may think it a happineſs, when a caſt created particularly for the exerciſe of the prieſthood, in reading, teaching, and performing the ceremonies of religion, will condeſcend to exerciſe functions inferior to theſe, whilſt none of the other caſts dare look up to theirs. Even that of the Raypouts, of which is the Raja, whoſe particular diſtinction is the profeſſion of arms, to protect the ſubjects by their valour, and who therefore naturally have command, is inferior to that of the bramins, who are by the people more reſpected than the prince.

Beſides

Beſides this ſpirit of the Gentoo ſyſtem, Seva was attached to the bramins by policy; to them he owed his firſt ſucceſs, and from their influence he hoped yet greater advantages. Of his bounty and munificence, as well as deference to them, inſtances have been related on occaſion of his coronation and marriage; whilſt therefore he retained the enſigns and reality of ſupreme dignity, the power of peace and war, the command of armies, the diſpoſal of employments, governments, and jaguiers, and the management of the public treaſure abſolutely to himſelf, he inſtituted a council of eight perſons choſen among the bramins to aſſiſt him in the adminiſtration of the civil government. They exerciſed the principal offices of the ſtate under him, they held theſe offices only during his pleaſure, in proceſs of time they perpetuated them in that caſt. Next in dignity to the Raja was the Purtenary, or delegate, whoſe fiat was previouſly neceſſary to all acts of ſtate: but the officer really moſt powerful was the Paiſhwa, or chancellor *; in him was the executive power of adminiſtration really lodged; and as the name imports,

* Fryer.

he presided over the council, and was the reigning, indeed sole, minister of the Raja. The spirit and activity of Seva Gi was such, that his ministers could assume little or no power: but as by him the independence of his tribe was settled, and the jaghedars fixed in their obedience and payment of their rent, his successors, like other Indian princes, yielding to the softness of the climate, and the allurements of luxury, to enjoy their pleasure left the administration to their minister. Similar causes produce like effects though in different climates; what happened in the first line of the French monarchy happened here; from the indolence and inactivity of the prince, the abilities and real service of the chief minister, the necessity to which the prince was reduced of being totally in his hands, the influence of the persons whom the minister had won over to second him, who in each state were rulers of the people's consciences, the power by degrees passed from the hand of the prince to that of the minister. The Mayor of the Palace, and the Paishwa, to the administration of government joined command of armies; success against foreign enemies confirmed them in that command; and the office fixed at firſt in their perſon for life only, in time became hereditary in their family, whilſt the prince became a mere cypher; and, ſatisfied with outward enſigns of royalty, led a life dependent on the will of him who had thus uſurped his authority. In this ſtate the Paiſhwa was aſſiſted by the reſt of the council, who ſaw by this change the government fixed in the bramin caſt; the office became hereditary, even when the Paiſhwa left an infant ſon, during whoſe minority the adminiſtration was veſted in a regent and the reſt of the council, and exerciſed in the name of the infant. The completion of this change was owing to the Raja Sahoo; in the beginning of whoſe reign a bramin called Wiſh-wana Ballagee, through his great abilities, ſeconded by dexterity, had ſo far gained his prince's favour and confidence, that he roſe to be of the Council of Eight, and ſoon to the office of Paiſhwa. The Raja, finding every day more eaſe from his management, determined formally to inveſt him with all his authority and power, and even ſome of the enſigns of royalty. From that time all orders formerly given in the name of the Raja iſſued in that of the Paiſhwa ſolely, whom Sahoo ſtiled Pundit Praden, chief or

elect

elect of the Pundits *. The only reſerve of this thoughtleſs prince was the revenue of a large diſtrict, from whoſe produce he maintained a conſiderable body of troops, who were his body guard, and ſolely under his command. From that time, ſhut up in Sattarah, and abandoned totally to his pleaſures, he appeared no more to his people, who, through the influence of the bramin caſt, were accuſtomed in a ſhort time to this alteration, which in reality had no bad effects to them. The bramins readily aſſiſted in a meaſure which fixed the government in their caſt, and gave a chance to each of their families of ſeeing the ſupreme power fixed in it.

This reſerve and guard makes it probable that by this ceſſion Sahoo did not mean to diveſt himſelf totally; his intention muſt have been only the attainment of perfectly undiſturbed tranquillity in the enjoyment of his pleaſures; but his abſence from buſineſs and the view of his people gave his ſubſtitute the opportunity of fully eſtabliſhing his power and influence, inſomuch that the office became not only permanent in himſelf, but

* Learned Bramins.

hereditary in his family: it is now an eſtabliſhed rule, the ſucceſſor goes to Sattarah, where the Raja reſides, and is inveſted in his office by the delivery of the ſirpaw *. Such a revolution muſt ſeem ſtrange, but it muſt be conſidered that the bramins who compoſed the council had, as moſt orders of men, the intereſt of their caſt principally in view: by this abdication they ſaw the government fixed in it, and each might hope that his own family would ſome time or other reap the benefit of it: and their influence over the people being ſo great, they eaſily brought them to ſubmit to any government they approved.

Wiſh-ana made uſe of his power in creating dependents, and by degrees ſo totally obſcured the Rajaſhip, that the prince became a mere image or repreſentative of royalty. As Sahoo muſt have been very weak as well as indolent and luxurious, it is not ſurprizing that, like the French monarchs, he was content with enjoying his pleaſures within his palace, and in time ſunk into a priſoner; probably his mind as well as his

* The ſirpaw is a rich garment with which the perſon who receives a great employment is inveſted in the preſence of the prince, or of the miniſter who carries it, if the favoured perſon is then abſent from court.

body

body enervated through ſenſual enjoyments, willingly acquieſced in this inglorious torpid ſtate. His ſecluſion from the world totally eſtabliſhed the empire of the Paiſhwa in the mind of his people, his perſon and his government were forgotten. Upon the death of Sahoo, he leaving no children, Raja Ram, who was only an adopted ſon, probably choſen by Wiſh-ana to ſerve his purpoſe, was permitted to ſucceed to this ſtate of captive royalty, and hath ever ſince acquieſced, and peacefully obeyed the dictates of the Paiſhwa or bramin council. The genius and circumſtances of the reſpective ſucceſſors of Sahoo and Wiſh-ana have ſo totally fixed the government in the Paiſhwa, that every tranſaction with foreign powers is merely between that officer and them, without any regard to the Raja.

Wiſh-ana's enterpriſing ſpirit did not long ſuffer him to reſt content with the incurſions uſually made by the Maharattas; he ſought to regain what the valour of the Portugueze, on their firſt invaſion of India, had wreſted from the inhabitants of that part of the Malabar Coaſt which lies between Surat and Goa: in a ſhort time he became maſter of the principal part of the coaſt, and by his own brother Oppah conquered Baſſein and Salcet. Theſe ſucceſſes encouraged him to attempt becoming a maritime power, and turned his thoughts to the eſtabliſhment of a marine.

The neighbourhood of this enterpriſing people made it neceſſary for the preſidency of Bombay to endeavour, by ſome treaty or agreement, to prevent any diſputes which might ariſe between them, and for that purpoſe one of their body was deputed to negotiate, who found the ſtate in the ſituation above deſcribed, and therefore treated with the Paiſhwa, by the intervention of Oppah, with whom ſundry articles were ſettled.

Wiſh-ana was peaceably ſucceeded by his ſon Ballagee, more generally known by the name of Nanah; during his adminiſtration the government was carried on with vigour; the military proweſs of the Maharattas eſtabliſhed a tribute, which, under the appellation of Chout, was exacted from all the countries ſouth of their dominion; the quarrels among the different princes calling them at ſome times to the aid of one; at others,

the

the non-payment of the Chout gave them a pretence of an irruption to gather the arrears; and thus continually employed abroad, and at home governing with firmness and justice, Nanah reigned without disturbance, and at his death in 1761, the power and post was transmitted, as of course, to his son Madharow, though he was then but fourteen years old. Ragonath * Row, the brother of the deceased Paishwa, carried on the government in the name of his pupil, and by his prudence conducted it so as to affirm the power of the Paishwa. The neighbouring princes, particularly the subah of the Decan, tempted by the youth of Madharow, invaded the territory of the Maharattas, but by Ragonath's activity and valour he was soon repulsed. His care extended to every part of administration; valour and conduct repelled foreign enemies; but internal evils were more difficult to be removed.

Wish-ana, on the first establishment of his power, as he was favoured by the rest of the council, to give it stability, found it necessary,

* Called also, and more generally by the English, Ragobah.

ſary, not only to employ them in the civil department, but to give them all the advantage of emolument that could ariſe from their offices; by this they were enabled to acquire great riches, and increaſe their intereſt, and that of the whole bramin caſt: his ſucceſſor continued the ſame manner; but probably Ragobah ſhewed ſome inclination to check this growth of power and wealth; for, during the minority of Mhadarow, they formed an intrigue, the effects of which have brought the Maharatta nation to ſuch a ſtate, that had any of the neighbouring powers been in a condition to take advantage of it, the whole muſt have been loſt. The bramins feared not only the diminution of power, and of the means of increaſing their riches, but the loſs of thoſe riches, always an object of jealouſy to the princes of that country. They ſaw the ſteady adminiſtration of the regent extended to every part of the nation, that his view was to affirm the power of the Paiſhwa, and make him independent of theirs; and from the talents of the young prince doubted not but, through his inſtructions, he would purſue the ſame plan, which muſt end in their ruin. It was neceſſary to prevent this, that Ragobah ſhould be removed. To effect

this

this would not have been eaſy, had not a favourable circumſtance offered the opportunity.

Nana had left a widow, who poſſeſſed the art of intrigue: ſhe was beſides a conſummate coquette; and, ſince the death of her huſband, had by her amours given great offence to Ragobah, who could not, without reſentment, behold ſo ſhameful a courſe of life; he reproached her for it; this procured him her inveterate hatred. The miniſters failed not to improve ſuch an advantage, and prompt her to uſe her influence over her ſon to the deſtruction of Ragobah. This was ſucceſsful: a coolneſs at firſt, was followed by an open breach, and total deprivation of power, and ended in Ragobah's confinement.

The ſucceſs of this intrigue at firſt threw the whole power into the hands of the miniſters; their rapacity knew no bounds; as they were the diſpenſers of favour, in a country where preſents make the firſt claim, they could not fail amaſſing immenſe riches, and greatly extending their intereſt by the opportunity they had of making creatures, at the expence of the Paiſhwa's treaſury. It happened

pened, that the northern jaghedars, feeing the weaknefs of government, with-held their tribute, and were in this followed by the Pundits; they purchafed, for a fmall part of what they ufed to pay, the protection of the minifters: fo the treafury vifibly diminifhed, while their ftores increafed. But this lafted not long.

As Madharow advanced to manhood, he fhewed all the talents which form a great prince, and put in practice the inftructions he had received from the regent. One of his firft cares, upon his taking in hand the reins, was to deftroy this iniquitous combination, by narrowing the power of the minifters, and reftoring that firmnefs of government which had exifted during the regency of his uncle; who, notwithftanding the Paifhwa's penetration, was ftill kept in his difgrace and confinement. The ability and activity of Madharow made him be refpected at home and dreaded abroad, and would certainly have proved as advantageous to his nation as fatal to his neighbours, had his life been longer. A lingering diforder put an end to his defigns in November 1772. He faw his end approach with firmnefs, yet with great anxiety

at

at the ſituation in which he left his family. His brother and ſucceſſor, Naron Row, was young and weak, confiding in thoſe who flattered his paſſions and vanity, and totally under the influence of his mother. The wiſe adminiſtration of Ragobah recurred to him. The contraſt between which, and that likely to be under thoſe diſadvantages, was ſtriking. Senſible that the good he had begun could be continued by him only, he wiſhed to throw the management of the ſtate into his hand. He knew the hatred of his mother, and the deſigns of the miniſters, the conſequence of whoſe ambition might loſe the Paiſhwaſhip to his family, if not extinguiſh the office: at the ſame time much was to be feared from the reſentment of Ragobah; ſome marks of which had appeared in his impatience at his confinement, projects formed for his eſcape, and meaſures taken to revive his intereſts among his friends; yet he knew him to be of a high ſpirit, and naturally, not only bold and enterpriſing, but alſo generous; and as he had no children, ſuppoſed he might look on Naron as his own ſon, and moved by the confidence repoſed in him, act as his friend and parent; he determined therefore to try that method; and calling to him his brother, ſhewed him the dangers that ſurrounded him from

from the ambition and avarice of the ministers, and the intriguing ſpirit, with the implacable temper of his mother: he then had Ragobah brought in, and after many kind expreſſions conjured him, forgetting the ill uſage he had received, to protect his nephew, and aid him with his councils; at the ſame time recommending to the young man to be totally guided by him, and to guard againſt the influence of his mother, and the ſnares of the miniſters: each promiſing what he requeſted, he joined their hands in token of mutual friendſhip and alliance. Soon after this he expired. The firſt acts of the young Paiſhwa, after the death of his brother, had the appearance of a determination to perform his promiſe. It was agreed that Ragobah ſhould be naib, or deputy, and carry on the adminiſtration of government in the name of Naron. In purſuance of this, when the Raja inveſted him with the ſirpaw of Paiſhwa, he conferred the naibſhip on Ragobah. Thus things wore the face of harmony; but the different intereſts of the perſons compoſing the cabinet, and the reſtleſs ſpirit of Gopicaboy *, who retained all her influence, ſoon deſtroyed it. The deceaſed Paiſhwa had

* The mother of Naron and widow of Nanah.

placed

placed great confidence in the Duan, Saccaram Bapoo, and recommended him to that of his ſucceſſor. But a young man named Nanah Furneze, who had attached himſelf to Gopicaboy, and whoſe age and diſpoſitions nearly approached Naron's, inſinuated himſelf in his favour, and formed the deſign of making it ſerve his ambition. His wealth, family intereſt, and connexions were conſiderable enough to create a ſtrong party, which, with the addition of Gopicaboy, became an overmatch for Saccaram: but Ragobah was an unſurmountable check to their deſigns, and therefore it was abſolutely determined to remove him from the perſon of Naron, and deprive him of his office. The ſame means which had effected this with Madharow were repeated; and a particular incident gave them a handle for their inſinuations.

Whether the weakneſs and debauchery of Naron had diſguſted Ragobah, or whether he was ſwayed by other motives, he, ſome time after the death of his nephew, had adopted a youth named Furrat Row, who was nearly related to Moodagee Bouncelo, one of the moſt powerful and conſiderable of the Maharatta chiefs. This adoption, and the connexion

nexion consequent to it, were by Gopicaboy used as strong arguments that Ragobah designed to establish himself in the office of Paishwa, to the prejudice of Naron. She represented that he had acted contrary to the custom of the country, which approved not adoptions where there were nephews; that by this the succession to his wealth was taken from his family; and perhaps the high office of Paishwa might be so: that the connexion with so powerful a chief as Bouncelo could have no other view but establishing such an interest as might overbalance the Paishwa's power. By these insinuations, and the flattery of Nanah and his young companions, the dying request of the late Paishwa, and promise in consequence, were obliterated, and Ragobah was once more a prisoner; and, on the 11th of April 1773, closely confined, and deprived of the access of his friends.

Naron, thus freed from the controul of his uncle, gave a full range to his folly; his debauchery, pride, and arrogance knew no bounds. The confidence was given totally to Nanah and his adherents, and Saccaram the Duan not only was neglected, but insulted,

ſulted, and even deſigns entertained of depriving him of the duanſhip. This Gopicaboy was labouring to effect, and her principles were ſo known, that it was not doubted but his life, if it ſeemed neceſſary, would be quickly ſacrificed to her thirſt of power and revenge. The apprehenſions riſing from this knowledge were ſoon encreaſed to certainty. By the means of Bouncelo, Saccaram received notice that a plot was formed to aſſaſſinate him and Ragobah; this, in a mind already inflamed, ſunk deep, and was followed by a reſolution to ſecure his own ſafety by any means. The moſt obvious was the death of Naron; this was inſtantly reſolved: but it was neceſſary to go further: ſeizing the power into his hands and that of his friends was the moſt deſirable, but whilſt the office of Paiſhwa exiſted, or Ragobah lived, this was not eaſy. The extinguiſhment of the office might reſtore the Raja, and deprive them and their caſt. The death of Ragobah would open the eyes of all, and repreſent their act, not as a meaſure of ſafety and public utility, but inordinate ambition. On the other hand, Ragobah, if releaſed, might look on them as his friends, and preſerve to them their wealth and power: thi[s]

determined

determined them to releaſe and reinſtate Ragobah. This ſcheme was laid, and carried into execution by the art of Saccaram, who prevailed on Mahomet Eſoof and Summer Sing to procure two Subadars to undertake the death of Naron: on the 18th of Auguſt 1773, they led their party, which conſiſted of five hundred men, to the Durbar, under pretence of being muſtered; the gates were forced, and the guards put to the ſword. Naron, rouzed by the tumult, ſaw the fullneſs of his danger, and at the ſame time the impoſſibility of eſcaping. The priſon, where Ragobah was confined, ſeemed the only refuge, thither he fled, and throwing himſelf at his uncle's feet, begged his protection; and aſſuring him nothing more than impriſonment had ever been deſigned againſt him, beſought him to aſſume the government, and only ſave his life. Before any thing could be anſwered, the party broke in, and found him in that poſture. Ragobah had time only to take him in his arms, which act would have ſaved him; but a ſlave, whom Naron had lately cauſed to be ſeverely whipped, and who had led the party to this apartment, urged them on; their weapons were inſtantly directed to the perſon of Ragobah, who,

who, to ſave himſelf, was obliged to abandon the wretched youth to their ſwords.

Thus did a moment determine the fate of theſe two princes. The one, who languiſhed in priſon when he expected death, was raiſed to liberty and command: and the other, in the height of ſecurity, fell a victim to his arrogance.

Ragobah was inſtantly brought out of his confinement by Saccaram, and by him and the other miniſters ſaluted Paiſhwa. His adopted ſon was ſent to Sattarah to obtain the inveſtiture of the office, with which he immediately returned, and Ragobah entered, in all appearance, peaceably upon the execution of it.

The conſpiracy againſt Naron had been kept ſecret to the moment of its execution: and as no life was ſought but his, Nanah Furneze, and his adherents, had time to ſave themſelves by flight. Ragobah recalled them, and, having given them aſſurances, they reſumed the exercise of their offices; Ragobah was acknowledged by them, and all the inferior offices throughout the Maharatta ſtate, and every thing ſeemed peace.

Mr. Moſtyn, the reſident of the Engliſh Company at Poonah, made him the uſual preſents, accompanied with a proffer of our friendſhip, which was accepted, and mutual engagements were entered into to maintain the alliance made with his anceſtor Badjerow.

But, though every thing at Poonah wore the appearance of peace and acquieſcence under this eſtabliſhment, diſſatisfaction and fear lurked in the Durbar, and in a ſhort time broke out to the diſturbance of the ſtate, and ruin of the Paiſhwa.

The miſchiefs which had ſprung forth during the firſt impriſonment of Ragobah, were but kept under in the ſhort adminiſtration of Madharow, and revived with more force than ever in that of Naron. Hence Ragobah, at his acceſſion, found an exhauſted treaſury, a ceſſation of the payment of tribute by the neighbouring princes, and the principal offices held by perſons attached to one or other of the parties which divided the Durbar. Both united in their ſentiments as

to

to him. Even Saccaram and his party were determined, if poſſible, to keep him in ſuch a ſtate, that he ſhould be dependent on them, or at leaſt not of ſtrength ſufficient to enable him to call them to an account for peculation and iniquitous waſte of the public treaſure. For their freeing him from impriſonment, and inſtalling him in the Paiſhwaſhip, was not owing to any affection for him or his family, but ſolely to the neceſſity of ſhewing ſomething of a regard to the public, which might cloak their intereſted views. Ragobah knew this well: he had already felt the effects of their cabals; but as he was now not under the power of any ſuperior, he did not fear influence; he therefore took the ſhorteſt method of mending his affairs and recruiting his treaſury, by requiring the payment of arrears of tribute from the princes of Indoſtan, at the ſame time managing the revenues of the ſtate by his own officers, without a duan or treaſurer: to bring the former meaſure to paſs, he applied to Modagee Bouncelo, that ſome of the force under him ſhould join the ſmall body he had on foot, and at the head of theſe he marched againſt the Nizam of the Decan, to bring him to pay the arrear due by him, and encamped in his territory. Though he knew the disposition of both parties against him, and from the nature of man must have concluded that Saccaram's disappointment, in not being Duan, must have made him a bitter enemy, he left Poonah, without proper precautions, accompanied by some of those very persons who dreaded his power, and feared, when thoroughly established, it would be turned against them. The consequence had nearly proved fatal to him: part of these retired from his camp, when in sight of the Nizam's army, and the other concerted measures to deliver him up to his enemy. They succeeded so well that in November 1773, when the Nizam's forces encountered him, having been, in the beginning of the action, surprized in his tent, to which the Nizam's troops had been suffered to pass, he narrowly escaped after receiving some wounds; a total defeat of his army followed. But as the nature of those troops prompts them soon to fly, so it saves many, who immediately again appear in arms; Ragobah was therefore soon again at the head of an army, which, by Modagee joining him, amounted to 60,000 horse; on the other hand, Shabajee, brother to Modagee, who disputed with him the

Rajaship

Rajaſhip of Berar, joined the Nizam with a force of 40,000. Ragobah having taken the fort of Muldroog advanced to Badar. The armies lay ſeveral days in ſight of each other; frequent ſkirmiſhes enſued: both parties ſuffered great inconvenience: Ragobah, from want of money, and the diſtruſt of thoſe who remained at Poonah; the Nizam from the great expence and the uneaſineſs on ſeeing two Maharatta armies in his territories: they were therefore eaſily brought to treat on the 9th of December 1773, and a peace was concluded. Ruckna al Dowla, the Nizam's vizir, promiſing on his behalf to pay twenty-five lacks of roupies *, and to cede ſome fortreſſes agreed on. This treaty was followed by an interview between thoſe princes, in which the Nizam having convinced Ragobah of his inability to pay the ſum ſtipulated; he, who wanted to ſecure the aſſiſtance of ſo powerful an ally, and expected much larger treaſures from the Carnatic, and the country of Hyder Ally, changed the terms of their treaty, and relinquiſhed the demand of the money, on the Nizam's undertaking to furniſh a certain number of troops whenever he ſhould demand them.

* About 250,000 l. at 2 s. the roupie.

Having finiſhed theſe affairs, he directed his march towards the country of Hyder, demanding the arrears of Chout, at the ſame time writing to Mahomet Aly Cawn nabob of the Carnatic, requiring his aſſiſtance. Having advanced as far as Cutberge, thirty coſs * weſt of Bedah, he was there met by Hyder's vaqueel, who immediately entered into treaty: Hyder paid down twenty-five lacks of roupies, and in return obtained the poſſeſſion of the diſtricts of Mudgwanny, Hanſcotah, and Chunda Groog.

Ragobah then turned his thoughts to the invaſion of the Carnatic, to demand arrears of Chout from Mahomet Aly; his army by his ſucceſs had increaſed, and the hopes of the plunder, which is ever the fruit of thoſe expeditions, had drawn to him a great number of horſemen. This boded deſtruction to that whole country, not only from the ravages of his troops, but an invaſion by Hyder, who would not have failed to take advantage of thoſe circumſtances. Fortunately for Mahomet Aly the attention of Ragobah was called off by the effects of the cabals at Poonah, to which his abſence had furniſhed an occaſion. The party which had ſo ſud-

* A coſs is nearly two miles.

denly changed the fortune of Ragobah, ſoon found that their hopes of his ſuffering them to acquire an increaſe of riches and power were vain. They remembered the ſteadineſs of his adminiſtration when regent, his determination to reſtore the power of his office, and prevent the miſchiefs which had given them ſuch influence and wealth; they now ſaw the firſt ſteps of the ſame plan, and with the more likelihood of ſucceſs to him and ruin to them; as he was not governing for another, but in his own right, all parties were equally intereſted to prevent the growth of this ſyſtem. The principal among them, Saccaram Bappoo, Nanah Furneze, Hurry Peut Furkia, Anunt Seva Gi, and another, united in a league, which they called The Five Friends: as the hazard was great, ſo the ſtroke was bold; they determined to deprive him once more of the Paiſhwaſhip and liberty, and ſeize the government. This ſcheme was thus brought about: Naron had left a widow called Gungaboy; it was given out that ſhe was with child, and the 30th of January 1774, ſhe was ſeized by them, together with another lady, wife of Sudaboy, a chief of the Paiſhwa race, who pretended to the regency, and whom they kept

 in

in confinement, and carried to the fort of Porounder, where five bramin women then with child accompanied her; thus they obtained a great probability that a male child ſhould be born in that fortreſs: till his production the government was to be carried on in the name of Gungaboy, they aſſuming no higher title than that of miniſters. Every perſon in the intereſt of Ragobah was put under a guard; and the Friends immediately levied troops to ſupport this uſurpation.

But notwithſtanding all their precautions Ragobah was informed of their proceedings, before their advices could reach the confederates they had in his army, and through whom they expected to ſeize his perſon: he ſaw his danger in the ſtrongeſt light; many of thoſe who ſurrounded him he knew to be of the bramin faction, and united with the miniſters, and he judged that the tale of the pregnancy of Naron's widow would ſeduce many more. His firſt care was to ſecure his perſon; he diſbanded his army, and retired to Gutty, a fort poſſeſſed by Mora-row Goparah, a Maharatta chief, who had great power and influence in that country, and commanded a conſiderable body of troops.

Fortunately

Fortunately he declared himſelf his friend, and not only afforded him a retreat where his perſon was ſecure, but promiſed him aſſiſtance to reduce this rebellion. An impolitic ſtep of the Five proved at the ſame time favorable to him. They too ſoon ſhewed the reality of their views by calling on all the chiefs to diſcharge the arrears they owed; this provoked many, and drove them to Ragobah, who by theſe means ſaw himſelf once more at the head of an army; that raiſed by the Five, commanded by Trimbuck Row, a chief of great reputation, was now marching againſt him; by the acceſſion of Shabagee's force it had increaſed to 60,000 men; Sindia, Holcar, and the Nizam joined in the league with the miniſters: ruin now ſeemed inevitable: nevertheleſs, as he had now an army in which he confided, through his opinion of Mora-row who ſupported him, he marched from Dalari on the ſouth ſide of the Khriſtna, and croſſing that river advanced towards his enemies. A body of troops from the Nizam had joined them, ſo that in all reſpects they were ſuperior to him. This inſpired them with a confidence of which he took the advantage: on the 24th of March he halted at Merits, a place within four coſs

of

of them; in the entrance of the night he placed a ſtrong party in ambuſh, and then decamped with all the remainder of his army, leaving his tents ſtanding, and all his heavy artillery: this apparent flight ſoon reached the ears of Trimbuck, who led the van of the enemy; he, fluſhed with the hopes of a victory ſo eaſily gained, haſtily marched in purſuit, without waiting for the Nizam and Shabegee who were in the rear: he met no oppoſition till he had paſſed the ambuſh; but then, to his great ſurprize, ſaw Ragobah marching ſwiftly to attack him in front; at the ſame time the corps in ambuſcade fell upon his rear. Trimbuck endeavoured by valour to repair the miſchief brought on him by his raſhneſs; but it was in vain: his army was totally defeated, he himſelf wounded, and taken priſoner. Ragobah now advanced toward Poonah. Holcar and Sindia, who had not ſent their quota of troops, though required by the miniſters, ſeemed to ſtand neuter.

The conſternation at Poonah was now great; ſtrongly impreſſed with the terror of the return of Ragobah at the head of a victorious army, it was once propoſed, as the only means of ſafety, to releaſe the Rajah, and

and reftore the antient form of government, by which proceeding they reckoned to fecure the adherence of moft of the Maharatta chiefs. But this was a meafure too replete of danger to themfelves; they muft have been called to account for all the ufurpations of their caft, which from that hour would be depreffed; lofs of wealth, perhaps of life, might probably follow. A few moments reflexion induced them to adopt a lefs dangerous plan, which the birth of a child in Porounder, offered them an opportunity of executing. On the 28th of April 1774 a male child produced, as born of Gungaboy, was called by the name of Madoo Row Narrain, and acknowledged as Paifhwa.

Although this contrivance was moft grofs, and attended with every circumftance of fraud, the firft report of pregnancy arifing fo confiderable a time after the death of Naron, the feizure of the widow, the ftrict care that none but their own confidential dependents fhould have accefs to her, a fence being erected round the fort for that purpofe, but above all the caufing her to be accompanied by five women with child, infomuch that it was, at the time of her confinement, publicly

licly called an artifice, and treated as ſuch by the Nizam in his propoſals for a pacification; yet, ſuch as it was, from its nature it kept many in ſuſpenſe, and enabled the contrivers not only to ſcreen themſelves, but maintain their power. The doubt that a ſon of Naron's might exiſt, detached the friends of the family from the intereſt of Ragobah, and the hopes of becoming conſiderable in the adminiſtration of perſons who muſt embrace every reſource that offered, and highly reward thoſe whoſe ſervices they needed, induced many, otherwiſe indifferent, to eſpouſe this cauſe. Ragobah was now within four coſs of Poonah, when, on the 13th of April 1774, letters from the Five Friends to Holcar and Sindia were intercepted by him. The matter and ſtyle of them was ſuch as led him to conclude that a correſpondence was eſtabliſhed between them, and that ſome bargain tending to his deſtruction was either ſchemed or actually begun. The infidelity naturally to be ſuſpected from Indian chiefs ſo ſeized his imagination, that he gave himſelf no time to examine whether theſe letters might not be an artifice of the faction, and were not purpoſely thrown into his hand: he therefore inſtantly

inſtantly determined to leave a place which teemed with ſuch danger, and have recourſe to the friendſhip of others. He immediately retreated with a body of a thouſand horſe, with which, on the 27th of May, he croſſed the Nerbudda, and ſeemingly directed his march towards Dehli, to which place his remaining friends imagined he would go; but when he reached Indoor, he turned ſhort, and joined Govind Row, who was then at the head of a conſiderable army actually carrying on the ſiege of Broderah. Govind promiſed to eſpouſe his cauſe, and if their forces had been joined, they would have found themſelves at the head of 40,000 men.

If the letters thus intercepted were a device, it ſucceeded even beyond the expectation of his enemies. Holcar and Sindia, if become adverſe to him, had thereby a colour for joining the cabal, and his flight making his affairs ſeem deſperate, they ſaw the faireſt opportunity of completing their defection. Accordingly a treaty was entered into between them and the Five Friends, who found it neceſſary to eſtabliſh their ſyſtem on a baſis more extended; and to intereſt the Rayput chiefs in their cauſe, which, when ſupported

ſupported by the joint intereſt of the bramins and warriors, would become immoveable. Holcar and Sindia, and five other Maharatta chiefs, were therefore aſſociated, and the whole called by the name of *The Twelve Friends*. The infant Narrain was by them acknowleged Paiſhwa, and the ſirpaw procured for him from the Raja. The principal article of agreement among the Twelve was, the total and perpetual excluſion of Ragobah from the government.

The remains of Trimbuck's army had been re-aſſembled under another general named Hurry Furkia, who joined the Nizam and Shabagee: they followed Ragobah in his retreat. Ragobah's officers preſſed him to attempt an engagement with them, hoping by a deciſive ſtroke to end a ſervice for which, in his circumſtances, he was not able to pay them, for his treaſures were exhauſted. This ardour made him ſuſpect their fidelity: on the other hand, the Nizam and Shabagee, though they did not ſeparate from Furkia, invented delays, their intention being not to put an end to the war, but harraſs Ragobah, and draw money from the miniſters. This afforded him time to make his retreat without

out loſs, and to deliberate upon his future proceedings. He did not chuſe to venture a battle, but directed his views to Brampour, hoping that when there he might be able to raiſe money; and that if Sindia and Holcar were well inclined to him, which he flattered himſelf might be, as the latter had received him in his retreat, and that both had quarrelled with the miniſters, they would have it in their power eaſily to join him; his project was then to return into Berar, till the enſuing rains ſhould oblige the Nizam to quit the field. And if he was not joined, but forſaken, to go to Sujah ul Dowla, the Nabob of Owde, under whom his brother ſerved in a conſiderable command.

Union could not long ſubſiſt among his enemies; each claimed a ſuperiority over the others. Some endeavoured to get Raja Ram, whom they kept confined at Sattarah, and who had no children, to adopt a ſucceſſor, whom they would have recommended; but this he refuſed.

This unſettled ſtate of affairs at Poonah not only gave Ragobah time to breathe, but opened the eyes of many who were originally well

well inclined to him, and encouraged ſome to aſſiſt him with their force. He was now at Indoor, where Holcar and Sindia ſent him conſiderable bodies of men. Govind Row was his declared friend; ſo that he was once more at the head of a numerous army. Hurry Furkia having left a conſiderable detachment near Poonah, marched with the remainder towards Aurengabad. Shabagee retired towards Berar; the Nizam in diſguſt withdrew, and remained till the rains were over at Dowletabad, which was to be delivered to him.

On the 27th of June, Saccaram, Nana, and Gungaboy, in the dead of night, flew precipitately from Sharpoor, where they were to have reſided during the rains, to Porounder: they pretended they had then found the truth of a treachery which they had long ſuſpected, that Morabah Batchiabah Bobbagee Naig, whoſe ſon had married Ragobah's daughter, were to have ſeized them: that Batchiabah was to have executed this ſcheme. Being diſcovered, he retired towards Jezeray: Morabah who, through his great intereſt among the people, thought himſelf ſecure, remained at Poonah; the others went

to

to Baramooby. During theſe troubles Hyder, Bugatta Jung, and Morarow Gopperah reduced the countries on their ſide of the Carnatic, and laid ſiege to and took ſeveral forts belonging to the Mahrattas.

Before theſe laſt events, however great the appearance of ſucceſs, Ragobah thought it prudent to ſtrengthen himſelf by an alliance with the Engliſh. In the month of Auguſt preceding, he, through his Vaqueel at Bombay, had made overtures for that purpoſe: the requeſt on his ſide was a body of troops; but the advantages he offered in recompence did not come up to what the intereſts of the Company and the repeated orders of the Directors obliged the council to require. The acquiſition of Salcet and Baſſein were the firſt, almoſt the ſole object; the ceſſion of either of theſe was what he could not then think of. The importance and revenue were great; the evident policy of that ſtate was to reſtrain within very narrow limits every power in the weſtern part of their dominions. The Engliſh from their ſtrength and reſources were of all others the moſt dangerous neighbours; and the bramins, by the honour of their family, were bound to preſerve the poſſeſſion of theſe territories; they made part of the particular demeſne of the Paiſhwas. The great Chimnagee Oppah had conquered them from the Portugueze, and it was the only exiſting conqueſt made by the natives of Indoſtan upon Europeans. Theſe reaſons, and the flouriſhing ſtate of his affairs, induced him to reject the conditions propoſed by the Bombay council, the principal whereof were the ceſſion of theſe two valuable poſſeſſions. They waited till time in its revolution ſhould offer the wiſhed-for opportunity: it was now come. The infidelity of ſome, the inconſtancy of others, and the continual dread of a reverſe of fortune, turned his thoughts towards the Engliſh, whom he now looked on as the only allies who would and could effectually aſſiſt him; he therefore now made a ſecond application to the council of Bombay, which, as he was in greater want of their aſſiſtance, contained offers affording a proſpect of attaining the long wiſhed-for poſſeſſion of Salcet. To judge properly of this tranſaction it is neceſſary to conſider the ſituation, circumſtances, connexions, and views of the princes who inhabited that part of Indoſtan. It hath been already

already mentioned that the Mahratta nation consists of many tribes governed by Rajas, acknowledging the sovereignty of the chief Raja, who resides at Sattarah, and paying a rent to him; in other respects they are like the ancient feudatories in Europe, independent; each governing his own subjects, being at the head of armies, and doing themselves justice upon any wrongs offered by their neighbours, but bound to a certain service when called on by the chief Raja, and furnishing a number of troops both to defend him against enemies, or to assist him in expeditions into the neighbouring provinces. Each of these princes actually maintains a considerable body of men, according to his means; these armies do not consist merely of real Mahrattas, but also of such adventurers as being destitute of possessions seek by soldiery to better their fortunes. If a man can purchase a horse fit for military service, he offers himself to some of the powers, whether Mahometan or Hindoo: thus their armies are soon formed. From the nature of such circumstances their chiefs are seldom united; each pursues the line which suits his interests, policy, or often passion or prejudice: their unions and separations are sudden and unexpected.

The moſt conſiderable of theſe chiefs, as well from the extent of his territory, as the number of his troops, was the Bouncelo. The Raja was then an infant, adopted for a ſon by the laſt Raja Jonnagee; he was his nephew, the ſon of his younger brother Moodagee, who, as father of this minor, claimed the regency; but he had a brother named Shabagee, who being elder than he, in that right claimed it alſo. Ragobah had eſpouſed the cauſe of Moodagee, and had beſides by his adoption of Furrut Ras ſtrongly attached him to his intereſt; the Five of courſe eſpouſed the cauſe of Shabagee. The embarraſſment of the affairs of theſe princes obliged them to remain neuter. The territory of this Raja extends from Orixa to Guzurat.

The Guycawars poſſeſs the whole Guzurat, and the country as far as Danaum. It was won from the Mogul by Pillagee, the grandfather of the preſent Raja; he held it for ſome time in independency, but Domulgee his ſon was by Nanah compelled to yield ſome places in it, to pay a rent, and bind himſelf to furniſh a certain quantity of troops when wanted. The revenues of their poſſeſſions amount

amount to eighty lacks of rupees, and their army to near 30,000 horſe. Inteſtine diviſions reigned in the family during the adminiſtration of Madoorow. Futty Sing had through his bribes to the governing bramins obtained the government; on the acceſſion of Ragobah he was by him deprived of it in favour of his brother Govindrow; this produced a war, which had ſo far turned out to the advantage of Govindrow, that Futty Sing was driven into Broderah, where he was beſieged by him.

Holcar and Sindia had conſiderable power; they had for a long time with-held the payment of their rent, and their view was to profit by the diſorders that reigned among the bramins; conſequently, though they had joined with the Five, and even become members of the confederacy, they had not continued that union, they found it to their advantage to act otherwiſe; policy requiring that Ragobah ſhould not be totally deſtroyed.

Morarow Goparah poſſeſſed the fort of Gutti, a ſtrong place, and alſo a very conſiderable diſtrict which bordered on the country of the Nizam. He had age and experience, and ſought principally the preſervation and quiet poſſeſſion of his jaghire, wiſhing to ſide with neither party, and watching the opportunity of making an advantage of the broils of his neighbours.

The real as well as apparent intereſt of the Nizam was, that the diſſentions at Poonah ſhould not ceaſe. He had already obtained advantages from Ragobah, by the ceſſion of ſome diſtricts, and had alſo received conſiderable ſums from the Five Friends.

The intereſts of Hyder were the ſame; he was buſied in reducing the forts yielded to him by Ragobah, and ſeemed rather inclined to favour his cauſe; but the probability was that he would aſſiſt neither party; yet his attention to ſeizeany advantage which might offer, made him much to be dreaded. He had lately ſtrengthened himſelf by an alliance with the Dutch, concluded with their ambaſſadors, Samuel Conſtantine and Charles Robert; the firſt article of which was a mutual engagement to aſſiſt each other againſt any power with whom each ſhould be at war; the force to be furniſhed by each in caſe of requiſition was ſettled, as was the pay

pay they were to receive; the governor of Batavia was to furnish this force.

By the eighth article Hyder required, that should Mahomet Ally, or the English, wage war against him, the Dutch should assist him with all the force they had in India; and if they desired to recover their country in Tanjore, he would assist them with all his force; the Dutch were to have the preference in his dominions for sandal-wood, pepper, cardamoms, and rice, for which they were to give iron and brass cannon, and all military stores.

The Company was at peace on every side: the war with the Rohillas concluded to their advantage; the settlement in Bengal in a flourishing condition; an army well disciplined, a treasury every day increasing, and the former errors of government and mismanagement of individuals almost obliterated.

Ragobah was now at the head of 40,000 horse; and such were the circumstances of the country round, when he applied for the assistance of the English, and in recompence offered the possession of Salcet, Bassein, and

 its

its territory, with the ſhare of the revenues of Surat that belonged to the Mahratta ſtate.

Such terms were what the Bombay council looked for; the attainment of them fulfilled the views of the Directors, and therefore they without heſitation accepted them. It was to be feared that, if refuſed, Ragobah would have had recourſe to the Portugueze, who would have gladly accepted even leſs. They had then lately been put upon a reſpectable footing by the increaſe of their military eſtabliſhment, and a great reformation in their government, and might have been of great ſervice to his cauſe. On the other hand the tranquillity of the Eaſt of India was ſecured; though gratitude ſhould fail, intereſt muſt bind Ragobah, the maintenance of his poſſeſſion depended on the continuation of the aſſiſtance through which it ſhould have been obtained: the total excluſion of the rivals of their trade in the dominions of this people; the accompliſhment of ſuch great ends, with honour, with juſtice, without bloodſhed, with the proſpect of ſecuring a peace through India, the execution of the repeated orders from England, the criſis, the only moment perhaps never to return, ſhould they

even

even hesitate; these were apparent. The Portugueze were watching the moment favourable to their repossession of those places. Their being conquered from them by Chimnagee Oppah in 1739, was not only a mortal blow to their trade and power, but a stain to their honour, and therefore the acquisition of them, whether by treaty or force, the constant object in view: if, upon the Bombay council's refusing or endeavouring to delay, Ragobah had applied to them, or if the distractions of the Mahratta state continuing, the so much wished-for occasion presented itself, they must have seized it, and a colour of justice would not have been wanting, since these dominions had been wrested from them so lately. This colour of justice the council of Bombay had not, nor could they, if once these possessions were resumed, grant aid to any Indian power to wrest them from the possessors *. Should the Portugueze neglect such an opportunity, and peace be restored

* The reforms then lately made in the management of the affairs of that nation had rendered them a much more respectable power than they had been; their marine was increased, both in number and the size of their ships; the Inquisition was abolished, and liberty of conscience given to all that settled at Goa or in its dependencies; the useless riches

ſtored to the Mahratta empire without the interference of the Engliſh, either by the deſtruction of Ragobah or that of his enemies, not only theſe poſſeſſions would not be ceded to them, but the collection of Chout would be renewed through all India. All parties are ready for an union on the propoſal of theſe expeditions: probably the province of Bengal, moſt undoubtedly the Carnatic, would have felt this.

The treaty concluded, ſuch troops as could then be ſpared were embarked for Surat, whence, as circumſtances ſhould permit, they were ordered to join the army of Ragobah. Theſe were 2500 men under the command of Colonel Keating. The plan was to aſſiſt in the reduction of Broderah, then beſieged by Govindrow; and, after hav-

riches of the churches were declared to belong to the king, and were applied to public uſes: the adminiſtration of juſtice was put on a firm footing, and carried on by perſons ſent from Liſbon, unconnected with the inhabitants of Goa; the ranks of the clergy and military ſettled; and that every thing might look to the encouragement of this ſervice, the denominations of that rank were taken from military names: thus a biſhop had the rank of a brigadier general. The force actually in Goa conſiſted of four regiments of infantry, amounting to 2240 men; one of marines, 800; three of natives, 2000; and 6000 ſepoys.

ing

ing put him in poſſeſſion of that important place, and thereby ſecured a friendly country in the rear, to march directly to Poonah.

This treaty, or the preparations in conſequence, could not be carried on with that ſecrecy neceſſary to ſecure the effects of them. Hurry Punt Furkia, one of the confederates, who commanded their army, was apprized of Ragobah's application, and determined to attack him whilſt the ſuperiority was on their ſide: he therefore, without loſs of time, directed his march to Broderah. This obliged Ragobah to raiſe the ſiege, and retreat to the Mahi, a river near Cambay. Futty Sing joined the confederate army; and, knowing the country, led them so expeditiouſly, that croſſing the Mahi, they came unexpectedly upon the center of the army of Ragobah. An action enſued, in which Ragobah for ſome time defended himſelf well, till, by a party of Arabs who had engaged in the ſervice of Govindrow, refuſing to charge, he thought himſelf betrayed, and quitting the field, retired with one thouſand horſe to Cambay. His general Phaukrea, with the beſt of his troops, retreated to the fort of Copperwange, about one hundred and fifty coſs

coss from Cambay, where Govindrow and Condah Row joined him. From Cambay, Ragobah proceeded to Surat, where the force sent from Bombay found him; here he ratified the treaty. His general gave him notice of his retreat to Copperwange, with his allies; of their safety and numbers, and of the possibility of effecting a junction with the English force should they advance to Cambay. Upon this it was determined our army should proceed there, the transport by sea was easy and secure; on the 18th of March they arrived, and proceeded to join the army of Ragobah. The confederate army lay between them; yet, by a motion happily concerted between the commanders, the English got possession of a secure post beyond the confederates, and a junction was formed on the 19th of April 1775. The whole of the army thus combined amounted to 37,500; of which 2500 were English troops.

Fortune, or rather the ill-timed rapacity of the confederates, once more favoured Ragobah. Deeming his ruin compleated by the last defeat, they hastened to fill their treasury. Orders were sent to Hurry Punt Furkia, their general, to seize Modagee Sindia, the jaghedar of Uguir, and send him to Poonah

nah to ſettle his accounts; he had intelligence of this, and knowing the conſquences of ſuch an impriſonment, he determined not to venture it, and ſuddenly left the confederate army with 12,000 horſe; the pretence was, that troubles had ariſen in his province, which his preſence was neceſſary to compoſe. Colonel Keating loſt no time in advancing towards the enemy, who, though ſuperior in numbers, carefully avoided an engagement, conſtantly retreating as he advanced, and ſometimes ſo as might be well termed flying. Ragobah had ſome particular reaſons to wiſh that our march ſhould be directed northward, but the deſtination and expreſs orders required that the march ſhould be to Poonah.

The confederates were ſtruck with the deſertion of Sindia; it gave them room to ſuſpect the ſincerity of Holcar, their other northern ally; the Nizam, notwithſtanding the ceſſions made, and ſubſidies granted by them, ſent no troops to their aſſiſtance; their ally Shabagee Bouncelo had been lately cut off by his brother Modagee; ſeveral chiefs, on whoſe aſſiſtance they had reckoned, now grew cold, and did not join them; probably,

probably, if Ragobah marched with victory to Poonah, would follow his ſtandard. The weight which the aſſiſtance of the Engliſh would throw into the ſcale, the extent whereof yet was uncertain; all theſe circumſtances determined the confederates to hazard an engagement; if they were victorious it would ſtop the current, and prepare the way for a negotiation with us, which Saccaram Bappo and Nanah Furneze were then meditating; if they were defeated, the ruin now inevitable was only accelerated. They therefore ſent orders to Hurry Furkia to riſk an engagement.

In every war, whether external or civil, there are inconveniencies on each ſide, which furniſh great advantages to the adverſary: experienced perſons know that they are inherent in the nature of human affairs, and from that experience conclude they exiſt: it was ſo here, Ragobah laboured under the want of treaſure; when he was ſurprized and forced to retreat to Cambay, all he could carry with him was the value of ſix lacks of roupies in jewels; the remainder of his valuable effects, which had not fallen into the poſſeſſion of his enemies, was ſecured in the fort

fort of Dhar, where his family had retired, and was not then within his reach. These six lacks were insisted on as a pledge of his performing his engagements to the Company. The resource of borrowing from the Shroffs or money-lenders at Surat could be but weak whilst his affairs stood in a precarious situation, his own security was not sufficient to procure their trust, and it was a step too bold for the council of Bombay to engage the credit of the Company: this distress was well known at Poonah; and that the Indian troops, if not paid regularly, or have not some prospect of immediate satisfaction, will not fight, or if they are brought to face the foe do it faintly; and the confederates hoped some advantage would arise to them from it during an engagement: any fortunate turn, the accession of some chiefs, would so change the aspect of affairs as to make these disadvantages vanish: this was another great incitement to their determination of hazarding a battle.

Ragobah's wish was to have penetrated northward to Ahmedavad, where he hoped to have procured money, which he stood so much in need of; but this scheme was soon found

found by Colonel Keating to be replete with inconveniencies, not only as it delayed the principal object in view, which was his establishment at Poonah, but from the nature of the march itself, as moving southward would oblige the enemy to follow, and the sooner bring them to an action: he therefore insisted on bending their march that way. This had its effect; the ministerial army followed, and on the 18th of May came up to the rear of the English, as they were at the entrance of a village where there were some defiles; their commander having expected this, his troops were very soon formed to receive them well, and though they attacked with great resolution, they were repulsed with a very great loss on their side, and very little on that of the English, till unfortunately the first company of European grenadiers, by an ill judged movement to the right retreated too precipitately from their ground; they were followed by the Madras infantry, and these by some sepoys; their movement, though too rapid, was regular till they reached some hedges with openings at intervals; crowding to get through these occasioned confusion, during which they were charged with success by a body of horse.

They

They then fled, nor could they be rallied, even by the commander himſelf; their flight having cleared the ground of them, the artillery played with ſuch ſucceſs on that body of horſe, that there remained not more than ten. This unfortunate motion was owing to an order given by the commander to ſeize ſome guns of the enemy, which muſt have been improperly repeated and ill underſtood: many officers were killed on that occaſion. This was the only loſs on the ſide of the Engliſh; that of the enemy was very great, the artillery having deſtroyed great numbers of men, horſes, and ſome elephants; many periſhed in their flight, and every day's news increaſed their loſs. Thus the event was fortunate to Ragobah, and ſo damped the ſpirit of his enemies, that the confederate army never from that time was brought to ſtand another attack; they retreated, without even making uſe of the advantage of many defendable poſts which the country offered. On the 19th of May Colonel Keating paſſed the Mahi in purſuit of them, but could not reach them till the 10th of June, when, at the paſs of Bowapier, they croſſed the Nerbedah; the Engliſh army there came up to their rear, which they attacked with ſucceſs: many were killed, their cannon were loſt in the river, and many men, horſes, and camels drowned; they retreated from thence with precipitation, leaving great quantities of provender and proviſion that they had not time to deſtroy; which, with ſome horſes and an elephant, fell into the purſuers hands: and thus the province of Guzurat was evacuated. To complete their misfortune, in their retreat, when they came to the Tappy, near Golow, it was ſo ſwelled and rapid, that in paſſing it they loſt a thouſand horſe. A little time before this the Mahrattas from Baſſein had made an attempt on Salcet, where they landed with 3500 men, but were repulſed with great loſs on their ſide.

The monſoons near approach made a further progreſs ſouthward dangerous: it was neceſſary therefore to ſuſpend that part of the operations; but what remained of the fair ſeaſon was employed in the reduction of Dubbay, a fortified place ſituated between Baroach and Broderah: this poſſeſſion produced conſiderable advantages. Our army could winter there, and the proximity of Baroach made it eaſy at the opening of the ſeaſon

ſeaſon for ſuch reinforcemonts and ſupplies as might be ſent from Bombay to join the army; thence the ſiege of Brodera might be eaſily undertaken. The poſſeſſion of that place was neceſſary to ſecure the country behind, when the army ſhould proceed to Poonah, the great object of the expedition. Other incidents then began to incline the balance to the cauſe of Ragobah, and the particular advantage of the Engliſh.

It hath already been mentioned that Futty Sing, one of the Gwicawars, had been appointed governor of the country of Guzurat by the confederates; as his advancement was owing to the money he had given them, he did not look on it as binding him to their cauſe, which he had eſpouſed ſolely with a view of preventing the ravage of his country; the ceſſions made by Ragobah to the Engliſh, ſhewed him things in a different light; he had, even at the time he joined the confederate army, made diſtant overtures to him, the retreat of Furkia made them ſerious and earneſt. The appearance of ſucceſs was totally on this ſide; if the reality followed it, all chance of his retaining any part of what he now poſſeſſed, was loſt; he had therefore recourſe to the mediation of the Engliſh, to whom he not only confirmed thoſe grants which Ragobah had made in the country under his government, but made further ceſſions to the amount of 178,000 roupies * a year. Through this mediation a treaty was made with Ragobah; Futty Sing ſubmitted to pay him the uſual tribute, and furniſh him the aid claimed by the Durbar of Poonah; and what was of moſt importance at that time, promiſed the payment of twenty-ſix lacks within the ſpace of ſixty days. Ragobah found means to ſatisfy Govindrow, and concluded this advantageous treaty of peace and alliance in the month of July 1775.

The proſpect of the affairs of the Company had not a leſs favourable appearance at ſea. In the beginning of the year the Mahratta officer who commanded at Geriah had equipped a ſquadron conſiderable for that country: it conſiſted of five ſhips; one of forty-ſix, two of thirty-two, and two of twenty-ſix guns, beſides ten Gallwats, or ſmaller veſſels, alſo armed. Commodore John Moore, with the Revenge and the Bom-

* 17,800 l. at 2 s. the roupie.

bay

bay grab, coming into these seas, immediately stood toward this fleet, which bore away; he ordered the grab to chace the admiral's ship, which was that of forty-six guns: the grab engaged her; this gave time for the Commodore to come up before she could run ashore: after an engagement of two hours the Mahratta admiral blew up, and was entirely destroyed; her commander and most of the crew perishing. The trade along the Malabar coast was now effectually protected.

The cause of Ragobah seemed now triumphant; besides the accession of Futty Sing, which enabled him to pay his troops, his friend and ally Moodagee Bouncelo now in full and undisturbed possession of his dominions, was advancing to join him at the head of a very respectable force. Ishmael Cawn was in march to join him with 4000 horse. Appagee Gunnis, who commanded at Ahmadabad, entered into treaty to surrender the place to him. The possession of this secured him from any enemy to the north of Nerbedah. A detachment was actually sent to receive it.

The confederates had made great advances to the Nizam to engage him to lend them aſſiſtance; they offered to cede to him the important fortreſs of Dowletabad with Burhampore Aſſery, and ſome diſtricts which the Mahrattas had conquered. Though he treated their pretenſions, and the infant Paiſhwa they had ſet up, with the greateſt contempt, the advantages offered were too great to be rejected; the poſſeſſion of theſe ceſſions once gained, a dexterous ſiding with the victorious party would confirm it. If fortune kept the balance even, whilſt it did ſo he was ſure of the continuance of this poſſeſſion; he therefore entered into treaty, and made a ſolemn engagement to aſſiſt them, and in conſequence they evacuated Dowletabad, and gave orders to their troops to withdraw from the other ceded places: but now he ſaw the time was come when to retain theſe he muſt abandon his new allies: the Engliſh having eſpouſed the cauſe of Ragobah, had changed the face of affairs: application was therefore made through the Nabob of Surat for the Nizam to be admitted into the alliance. He required the confirmation of what had been ceded to him, and that the Engliſh ſhould guarantee this poſſeſſion;

poſſeſſion: in return he offered his whole force, conſiſting of 50,000 horſe, 15,000 ſepoys, and a train of artillery: at the ſame time he ſent his vaqueel to Ragobah to propoſe a general accommodation on this plan, that Ragobah ſhould enjoy all the honours of the Paiſhwaſhip, and ſufficient revenues to maintain his dignity, that the government ſhould be carried on in the name of his adopted ſon Furrat Row, that the adminiſtration ſhould be in Marabah Furneze as Duan, and the confederates fully pardoned, and ſecured in the poſſeſſion of their effects, and the ceſſions, as juſt now mentioned, were to be confirmed to him.

As the cauſe of Ragobah advanced, that of the confederates declined. Sindia and Holcar had deſerted them, and the loſs of their aſſiſtance was a fatal blow, for on that they principally depended. Nanoo Oppah governor of Poonah, whoſe reputation and private character gave their party credit, was dead: Morabah Furneze who was one of the miniſters, and a man of conſideration, had not from the beginning joined the confederacy, though he had ſubmitted to act under the government it had eſtabliſhed: and yet, ſo much were they afraid of his influence, that they left him unmoleſted. Shabagee Bouncelo * was no more, and death had taken from them another very uſeful friend in the perſon of Ruckna ul Dowlah, the miniſter of the Nizam, to which accident they attributed his leaving them, and treating with Ragobah. But the union of the Engliſh was the moſt fatal ſtroke; reſiſtance to this was by moſt of the confederacy conſidered as vain in the end, and this deſpondency, which made each man ſolicitous for his own ſafety, and anxious for ſecurity of his perſon and wealth, made him ſuſpicious of his neighbour, and deſirous to prevent him in treating either with Ragobah or his allies; add to this, that from the known rapacity of the bramins, their ſucceſs was dreaded, even by their friends; that vice had infected and depreſſed their affairs from the beginning. The ſeveral Mahratta chiefs who had been drawn to ſupport their cauſe by promiſes of large ſums, were fruſtrated: the

* There was a conteſt between Shabagee and Monagee; a battle enſued; in this Monagee was defeated and taken priſoner, and the next morning Shabagee was found dead in his bed: Monagee was reſtored and proclaimed Raja of Berar.

public

public treaſure leſſened by their partial management, and now exhauſted by what they had ſent the Nizam, could furniſh no more; and though the bramins had great ſums of their own, their avarice overcame their policy, and prevented their ſacrificing any thing to the common cauſe; each, when applied to, referred to the treaſure expected from the Sircars. The nature of their troops prevented their being relied on when oppoſed to regulars with a well ſerved artillery; for each man had two fears, that for his horſe being as ſtrong as for himſelf, and as they are continually clamorous for their pay or other reward of ſervice, the greateſt advantage may often be loſt for want of a ſufficiency to ſatisfy them. Furkia was ever in dread of ſome accident of this kind; he ſaw the diſſatisfaction among the chiefs, and every moment was at the eve of being forſaken, perhaps ſeized and delivered up to the enemy. This had induced him, even in his flouriſhing ſtate, to try diſtant overtures for peace; during his retreat the evil increaſed, the men who had loſt their horſes openly complained, and demanded their pay of their leaders, who in their turn preſſed their commander: to ſatisfy their demand was impoſſible;

poſſible; though he had received bills for fifteen lacks of roupies from Poonah, the Shroffs refuſed to anſwer them. His deſign was to have marched to the northward, where he would have been at hand to watch the operations of the allies in the opening of the campaign; but the army refuſing to follow, he had been obliged to change his route, and march to Poonah: his army amounted to between twenty and thirty thouſand horſe and foot. In his way he paſſed through Holcar's country, who refuſed to advance any money, and under pretence that the death of Sujah ul Dowlah * made his preſence neceſſary in his jaghiere he totally and avowedly withdrew his troops. Saccaram Bappoo and Nanah Furneze had ſent Vaqueels to Bombay to treat of an accommodation: the Vaqueels were to treat jointly; one of them fell ſick on his arrival; before he recovered, the preſident was attacked with illneſs, and it was not thought proper to break through the common forms which might have ſhewn too great an eagerneſs, eaſily conſtrued into fear, the idea of which might have given

* Sujah ul Dowlah was the Nabob of Owde, a province bordering on the poſſeſſions of the Company, and lying between them and the Mahratta country.

them

them a confidence and encouragement to insist on better terms than what were the ultimate end of their commission; which, though they had not yet declared, were, on good ground, supposed to be principally security for the persons and wealth of the confederates, and perhaps some private advantage for their immediate employers.

Thus all tended to the establishment of Ragobah, and the reduction of his enemies: this sudden transition from a state of wretchedness to that of prosperity was totally owing to the English having avowedly espoused his cause: a respect for their power, and a confidence in their faith, had induced the neighbour chiefs to follow that party, and make them guarantees of the performance of the treaties they entered into under their mediation: the prosperity and honour of the Company was fully established in the West as in the East of Indostan, when the exertion of the authority placed in the governor and council of Bengal, by the act of parliament passed in the year 1773, almost totally ruined the fair edifice so fortunately hitherto erected.

The news of the treaty with Ragobah, and of the march in consequence, arrived at Calcutta the latter end of May 1775. Far from meeting with the approbation of the governor and council there, it was condemned by all as a measure impolitic, unjust, and unauthorized; impolitic, as throwing the burden of the war on the Company; unjust, as no injury had been received from the Mahratta state; and unauthorized, as the act of parliament vested in the Supreme Council the authority of treating with the powers of Indostan. The manner of carrying on the war in consequence of the treaty was no less reprobated than the treaty itself. Sending the Company's troops at such a distance from Bombay was called a rash step, which might be attended with fatal consequences. The governor general, in his minute of the 31st May 1775, painted these supposed evils in a very strong light, though at the same time he presented many difficulties attending the execution of any orders they might give in consequence of this reprobation; and therefore professed that he was much embarrassed in his choice of what measures might be most proper to be taken. That as things could not be replaced as they originally stood, so the distance

diſtance they were at prevented them from knowing the exact ſituation of them at that time; that it might be ſuch that the withdrawing our troops from Ragobah might be attended with many difficulties, perhaps dangers. He therefore propoſed that the preſident and council of Bombay ſhould be enjoined to cancel the treaty with Ragobah, and withdraw the detachment within the lines of the Engliſh poſſeſſions, unleſs it ſhould appear, in the firſt place, that they had obtained ſome conſiderable advantage; or, ſecondly, that it ſhould be dangerous to recall the detachment; or, thirdly, that a negociation ſhould have taken place between Ragobah and his opponents.

Mr. Barwell concurred with the governor general in the exception propoſed, and voted againſt the recall of the army; but General Clavering, Colonel Monſon, and Mr. Francis were totally againſt any exceptions whatſoever; and it was voted by that majority, that the treaty ſhould be cancelled, and the troops abſolutely recalled. It was determined to enter into a direct negotiation with the party at Poonah, and to ſend Colonel Upton to treat with them in the name of the Supreme Council:

Council: the purport of the inſtructions to be given to him was, in the firſt place, to expreſs a regret for the hoſtile meaſures adopted by the council of Bombay in concurrence with Ragobah, the Supreme Council's diſapprobation of that treaty, their deſire of re-eſtabliſhing a ſincere and laſting peace, to excuſe the ſeizure of Salcet as a meaſure only to prevent its falling into the hands of the Portugueze, and to alledge the impoſſibility of reſtoring it without the permiſſion of the Directors, to inform them of the orders given for the withdrawing our troops from Ragobah, and to endeavour to include him in the treaty.

In the mean time letters were written to Saccaram Bappoo at Poonah, announcing the departure of Colonel Upton, expreſſing a diſapprobation of the meaſures purſued by the council of Bombay, and informing them of the orders given in conſequence. Saccaram was an extraordinary perſon; he had riſen from an original ſtate of poverty, which prevented the firſt rudiments of education, by a natural addreſs which ſupplied that want, he had by degrees advanced his fortune ſo as to attain the principal offices of the ſtate, his

his experience ſeconded his talents, but not knowing how to write or read he was obliged to make uſe of and truſt others. His principal confidant was a bramin called Lalar, who had been governor of Concan, a province including Salcet and Baſſein, and had reaſon if that party prevailed, to hope a return to that government. Saccaram knew the true intereſts of the Mahratta ſtate, and therefore was naturally averſe to any ceſſions of territory, and every meaſure which could tend to give power and ſtrength to the Engliſh; this inclination muſt have been greatly ſtrengthened by the repreſentation of Lalar, who, by the ceſſions propoſed, would be ſo great a loſer; this letter was therefore too favourable to their views, not to produce great effects. The firſt was, freſh inſtructions immediately ſent to their Vaqueels at Bombay, which arrived before they had declared in form the purport of their miſſion: this now appeared very different from the humility which accompanied their firſt application: they demanded that the perſon of Ragobah ſhould be delivered up to them; the reſtoration of Salcet, and other acquiſitions which were then in actual poſſeſſion of the Engliſh; and the relinquiſhing all thought of of Baſſein, in return for which they condeſcended to defray the charge and expence hitherto incurred: yet at this very time, in all reſpects, other than the change likely to happen by the reſolution of the Bengal council, the affairs of the confederates were in a ſituation almoſt deſperate; Morabah Furneze had ſent a truſty perſon to Ragobah with aſſurance, that he and four of the moſt powerful men at Poonah were ſtrongly attached to his intereſts; and information that Fuikia was at Aurengabad, having ſcarce 5000 men under his command; that the whole force of the confederates did not exceed 12,000, and thoſe not eaſily aſſembled, or worthy of dependance on them; that Saccaram and Nanah Furneze had ſecured themſelves in Porounder fort, fearing to go from it; that Morabah himſelf was actually collecting a force from the troops lately paid off by the confederates, which he doubted not, by the time the allies could aſcend the Gauts *, would amount to 10,000 horſe, with which he would join Ragobah, and carry him without bloodſhed to Poonah. At the ſame time the news from the ſouthern parts were equally

* Gauts, Goats, or Gattes, are paſſes through the mountains.

favourable:

favourable: Beesi Sing, the Raja of Marwar, sent his Vaqueel with information, that he was on his march to join him, that he was within forty-five coss of Aurengabad, and that his force consisted of 10,000 men.

The council at Bombay were struck with amazemement at the resolutions of the Supreme Council, and the celerity with which they acted in consequence. They deputed Mr. William Taylor, one of their body, to Calcutta, to represent the motives which had induced them to act; the consequences of what they had done; the happy situation of the affairs of the party they had espoused; the benefits that would result to the Company from the cessions stipulated by their treaty with Ragobah; the danger of reducing him to despair, by abandoning his cause; the disgrace that would attend a breach of a treaty so solemnly made; and the necessity they were under to make it, if they would obey the orders of the Directors to omit no occasion that should offer of getting Salcet and Bassein into possession.

Mr. Taylor arrived in the beginning of October 1775, and, on the 9th, presented a memorial to the Governor and Council, representing these several matters, and proving the fatal consequences of sending any person directly from Calcutta to Poonah.

After defending the measures of the Bombay council, by shewing the advantage accruing from this treaty, and the necessity of acting in conformity to the orders of the Directors, the danger attending the alteration of measures, and forsaking Ragobah, from the circumstances of the neighbouring princes; the disgrace necessarily following the breach of a treaty, which, though perhaps rescindable by the Supreme Council, if the settlement by the late act of parliament was such as to invalidate in every case, the acts of subordinate presidencies when not confirmed by that council; yet as to the powers with whom it was made, unacquainted with these new arrangements, and confident that when they treated with the Bombay council, they treated with the Company, must be looked on by them as having force, and not to be rescinded without a breach of good faith; the policy of keeping up the present mode of administration in Poonah without running the hazard of having the bramins dispossessed, which might happen if by by the deſtruction of Ragobah that party ſhould want a chief, and muſt end in re-eſtabliſhing the Raja in power, and put an end to all diſſention, the conſequences of which muſt be fatal to the peace of all the reſt of India.

That as the letter written to Saccaram was worded, implying that the Supreme Council were unacquainted with the acknowledgment of Ragobah as Paiſhwa previous to the treaty, it left it yet in their power to chuſe what meaſures they would take; he therefore entreated them to warrant and aſſiſt the council of Bombay to fulfill their engagement with the Paiſhwa, as the only ſafe and honourable expedient in this juncture, and probably the laſt opportunity of attaining the end propoſed by the Directors, and eſtabliſhing the affairs of the Company on a firm and ſolid baſis. But whatever might be their ultimate reſolve, as to treating at Poonah, he moſt earneſtly recommended that the orders for withdrawing the army from Ragobah ſhould be revoked; it would have at leaſt this good effect, that all parties would be kept in ſuſpence until it ſhould be finally known, whether the preſent conteſt ſhould be decided by treaty or arms; it would prevent the bad consequences of a desertion of Ragobah, which must be that of his allies, and inevitably of the English; that whatever judgment might be formed of the origin of the measures, even though the council had unnecessarily engaged in a war, yet the continuance of it, as things stood, was necessary to the safety of the Company. If it should be objected, that this war was a violation of engagements formerly entered into with the Mahratta state, and of a neutrality recommended by the Directors, the answer was plain: these engagements being with the acknowledged chief of that nation and its legal representative, could not be a violation, but were in truth a continuation of the old; that on one side honour, acquisition of revenue, and influence in the first state in India, must be the consequence of pursuing the enterprize; on the other weakness, disgrace, and ruin must follow the retreat of the army before the accommodation which settled the interests and secured the safety of the several parties should have taken place. Before Mr. Taylor presented this memorial he had conferences with the Governor General, and each of the members of the

the council. The Governor, whose long residence in and experience of the affairs of India, made him a more competent judge, was soon convinced that the step was precipitate; Mr. Barwell joined with him. Indeed he had from the beginning opposed the withdrawing of the army; but the three members lately arrived from England had adopted a principle of peace in all events, and therefore over-ruled every expedient proposed by the Governor for complying in some measure with the representation of Mr. Taylor, and so determined was their resolution, that an answer was returned to his memorial the very day it was presented. All these things happened in October 1775 *.

In consequence of the resolutions taken by the Supreme Council, positive orders were sent to the council of Bombay, that the English army should immediately withdraw within the limits of the Company's possessions; that if Ragobah desired a retreat, they should afford it him; that until the treaty should

* It may be proper to place in one view the several places ceded to the Company by the treaty between them and Ragobah, with their produce to the Company.

 Salcet,

ſhould be ſettled between Colonel Upton and the government at Poonah, they ſhould retain the poſſeſſion of Broach, Coriab, Chicker-

		Rs.
Salcet, Caragah, Elephanta, Hog Iſland, and Canary produce a year —		350,000
Baſſein, with its dependencies, —		400,000
Oipad — — — —		350,000
Jamboſier — — —		400,000
The Gwicawars Share of Broach		350,000
To be paid annually from Occlaſier		75,000
Total Roupies		1,925,000
Which, at 2s. the roupie, is	L. 192,500	
and at 2s. 3d. the common exchange, is	L 216,562	
Preſented to the Company ſince the treaty by Ragobah, and Futty Sing on the concluſion of their treaty,	Rs.	
Coriab, near Broach,	50,000	
Chickely, near Surat,	100,000	
Veriow, near Surat,	28,000	
Ahmood, adjoining Broach,	150,000	
		328,000
Total ceded for ever		2,253,000
Remaining ſecurity for the payment of the ſubſidy		L. 225,300 at 2s. or L. 253,442 at 2s. 3d.
Remainder of the revenue of Occlaſier	Rs. 110,000	
Hanſoot — —	127,000	
Verſaw — — —	100,000	
Total ſecurity	337,000	

ley,

ley, and Verſaw, but carefully avoid all hoſtilities with the Mahratta army. Colonel Upton was to perform his journey to Poonah by land. Though this was to take up a great length of time, no inconvenience was foreſeen, as it was ſuppoſed that, upon a ceſſation of arms, every thing would remain quiet and in the ſame ſtate, and that paſſports, as well as conveniencies of travelling, would be procured for him during his whole route by the proviſion of the Poonah government. The Colonel ſet out on the 10th of July 1775, with a proper accompaniment, having with him Captain Allen Macpherſon, Sir James Paterſon, Dr. Sutton Banks a phyſician, and Captain Benjamin Wroe: and on the 24th of September had proceeded as far as Benares: he there received letters from Saccaram, the contents whereof gave him no great encouragement; and whoſe ſtyle was ſuch, that he complained of it to the Supreme Council, who thereupon wrote to Saccaram; and at the ſame time to the colonel, that he ſhould take advantage of the ſituation of the army under Colonel Keating, by telling the Poonah miniſters, that it now remained inactive near Surat, but that it ſhould act according to their behaviour; if they made any motion with their troops, that army ſhould likewiſe move, and the Supreme Council would not think themſelves bound to keep terms of amity with them: that as the Council meant to act with good faith, they expected the ſame treatment in every inſtance.

The earneſtneſs of the Engliſh for peace had appeared plainly in the beginning; for the ceſſation of arms had been publiſhed, and taken place in the month of Auguſt; and now, notwithſtanding the preſſing inſtances of Ragobah, that the army ſhould not yet withdraw from him, as it would produce ſuch a coldneſs amongſt all his friends, who would give up his cauſe as loſt and himſelf as ruined that he ſhould be immediately abandoned by them, the army, on the 20th of October 1775, began its march from Dubbay to retire into the Pergunnah of Surat; and on the 13th of November were within ſixteen coſs of that city. Ragobah dared not remain without their protection, and therefore with his troops followed their march; with hope, that from the repreſentations made at Calcutta, the Council might be yet induced to favour his cauſe.

The

The Nabob of the Carnatic, fearing the inroads of the Mahrattas when once they ſhould enjoy peace at home, deſired to have a ſhare in any treaty which ſhould be concluded by Colonel Upton with them; and for that purpoſe that he might ſend a Vaqueel to Poonah; the Council conſented that Mr. Chambers ſhould go from him to be aſſiſtant to Colonel Upton in what regarded his intereſt; but he was not to treat himſelf with the miniſters, or act in any other manner than through the Colonel, who alone was to manage all matters with them. Colonel Upton in proceeding on his journey did not find the effects expected from that readineſs in the Poonah Durbar, which the majority of the Supreme Council flattered themſelves with. On the 25th November he wrote from Bopaul, which is ſeventy coſs from Burhampoor, that he met many obſtacles; that the country was in arms; that he had yet received no paſſport from Poonah; at the ſame time the miniſtry wrote to the Supreme Council, that they had given orders for having every thing prepared, ſo that Colonel Upton might have a free paſſage; but that they had not then heard of his approach. The ſtyle of this letter ſhewed no pacific inclinations; they complained that the Bombay council;

council had not been attentive to the orders received from the Supreme Council; that they ſuffered the army under Colonel Keating to act offenſively; they found fault that Engliſh ſhips ſailed from place to place in their dominions, as if there was a full and entire peace eſtabliſhed between the two nations; they threatened to intercept them by means of the Mahratta fleet, and to ſhut their ports againſt them, and that if the places which had been taken by the Engliſh were not immediately reſtored, they would ſet their army in motion to recover them.

The complaint of hoſtilities was without foundation. Colonel Keating had, on the 20th of the preceding October, begun his march toward Surat; and at the very time this letter was written, had already reached its neighbourhood. Yet, notwithſtanding this boaſting, the Poonah miniſtry were far from being in a condition to ſupport this arrogance; for by Colonel Keating's intelligence, it appeared that Morabah Furneze * had embraced the party of Ragobah, that the miniſterial army was reduced to 12,000

* Furneze is a title of honour, it means one in receipt of the revenue.

men,

men, that they themſelves were in ſuch apprehenſion for their ſafety, that they had retired to the fort of Porounder, and were afraid to truſt themſelves out of it: and that Ragobah's partizans in Poonah were increaſing.

Ragobah himſelf required that Colonel Upton ſhould, in the firſt place, procure ſome diſtricts to be aſſigned for the maintenance of him and his adherents, till the final concluſion of the peace: that his pretenſions to the Paiſhwaſhip ſhould be fully diſcuſſed, by an examination of every thing relating to the birth of the infant pretended to be the ſon of Naron: that if he ſhould prove to be really ſo, then he ſhould, as his relation intitled him, be regent during his minority; and that when he attained his majority, and the regency was at an end, he ſhould have a penſion ſufficient to maintain him according to his rank.

After a tedious and difficult journey Colonel Upton arrived at Poonah, on the 30th of December 1775. Though he was at his arrival received with great civility, yet in a ſhort time he found he had to deal with people not only inimical, but uncertain; inſomuch,

ſomuch, that in the beginning of February he had no hope of concluding any thing with them. The detail of what paſſed between him and them from that time to the concluſion cannot be intereſting. After many entanglements got over, at laſt, on the 1ſt of March 1776, a treaty was ſigned at Porounder by Colonel Upton, on the part of the Company, and Saccaram Bappoo and Ballagee Pundit, on that of the infant Paiſhwa. By this it was, in the firſt place, mentioned, that peace between the Company in general, and the Bombay council in particular, and the infant Paiſhwa and his miniſters, Saccaram and Ballagee, on the part of the Mahrattas ſhould be fully eſtabliſhed. That this peace on each ſide ſhould be forthwith proclaimed. That the Mahrattas being anxious to recover Salcet, would in return give the Company a country producing three lacks of roupies, in the neighbourhood of Broach; but it was to be left to the option of the Supreme Council whether or no to accept this equivalent. The advantages to the Engliſh were:

1ſt. All right to the city and pergunnah of Broach was to be ceded to the Company free from all demand whatſoever: they were to have likewiſe a country of the yearly produce

duce of three lacks adjoining to Broach, the bounds whereof ſhould be determined by two perſons for the Company, and two perſons for the Mahrattas: and for the expences of the war, the Engliſh ſhould be paid twelve lacks; ſix within ſix months, and ſix within two years.

In return for this, all and every part of the Guzurat country which had been ceded by Ragobah to the Engliſh (that only ſettled on them by this treaty excepted) was to be reſtored; and all the country ceded by Futty Sing to the Company was to be given up to the Mahrattas, upon their producing proofs by the letters and ſunnuds * of the Paiſhwas, that Futty Sing was not authorized to make ſuch a ceſſion. Beſides,

All treaties made by the Bombay council with Ragobah were declared to be annulled, as was alſo that with Futty Sing. In conſequence the Engliſh troops were immediately to march within the limits of their preſidency. Ragobah was to diſband his army, and all his adherents but four (who were by name excepted) were to have a full and free pardon;

* Sunnud is a grant under ſeal.

if

if he refuſed to diſband, the Engliſh were to give him no aſſiſtance, but withdraw from him; and in conſideration of his diſbanding he was to have a train of a thouſand horſe, and a proportional number of foot, which ſhould be paid by the Poonah government, as well as two hundred domeſtics; and he was to receive three lacks of roupies a year, by monthly payments; but he was to reſide at Coopergunge, and not change his reſidence without licence from the Paiſhwa. The Engliſh were not to aid or aſſiſt in any manner, either Ragobah or any perſon diſturbing the peace of the Mahratta dominions: theſe covenants were to be mutual *.

Theſe are the material articles of this treaty which was ratified at Bengal, by the reſolution of the majority; the preſidency of Bombay made very ſevere ſtrictures on it, which they forwarded to Bengal. Ragobah looked upon it as his ruin; the fixing of his

* The advantages to the Company by this treaty were in point of revenue as followeth;

Salcer — — —	350,000	
City and pergunnah of Broach	500,000	
Country adjoining to Broach	300,000	
	1,100,000	L. 110,000 at 2s.

reſidence

residence at Coopergunge he considered as an imprisonment, and the thousand horse, and proportional number of infantry which were to be paid by the Poonah government, as a guard set upon him, either to keep him in that prison, or deliver him to their paymasters; and he declared, that it was better for him to try his fortunes with the few friends that might remain firm to him, than submit to accept such terms. He asserted, that confiding in the protection of the English nation, he had rejected offers made to him by the Nizam: he desired that he might make his appeal to that nation, and in the mean time take shelter in Bombay, that his person might be in safety.

There was some reason for Ragobah to have entertained hopes that his condition would have been better than it proved in the treaty: for not long before the conclusion of it Colonel Upton from several untoward circumstances, supposed the negotiation totally broken off, and had written his opinion to the Supreme Council, who, concluding it really so, had in consequence written to Bombay, that they might in that case be prepared

prepared to renew hoſtilities, and had alſo written to Ragobah, promiſing in that event an effectual aſſiſtance to reinſtate him. They had beſides applied to ſeveral other princes, Hyder, the Nizam, Modagee Bouncelo, Sindia, and Holcar, to ſupport his cauſe; if they declined this, intreating them to remain neuter. At the ſame time they had concerted meaſures with regard to Owde, and ordered a brigade to march to the frontiers of Corah, neareſt to the Paſs of Culpy; but all this was put an end to by the ſigning of the treaty.

Another accident which happened about that time helped to raiſe his hopes whilſt it embarraſſed the miniſters. There was a perſon of the Paiſhwa race, called Subahi, or Subadah, the ſon of Chimnagee Oppah and brother of Badgeerow, who was reported to have been killed in a battle near Panniput in 1761. A long time after a man appeared at Poonah, who aſſerted he was that identical Subadah or Subahi: he produced many proofs of that identity, but the government at that time looking upon him as an impoſtor, had confined him in the fort of Rutnah Geriah. This man had now eſcaped from thence, was joined by ſeveral chiefs with ſome troops, and

and Row Dullop who commanded the Mahratta fleet, had declared for him; he claimed to be regent either ſingly or jointly with Ragobah. Theſe circumſtances might induce Ragobah not yet to diſband his troops; a more ſpecious reaſon was given, that he had not money to pay them. He followed our army with them when they marched from Dubbay; and now they had moved to the environs of Surat, it was thought neceſſary, with the troops lately under Colonel Keating's command, to reinforce the garriſons of Surat and Broach, leſt ſome accident ſhould happen from ſuch a neighbourhood. Whether this excited a jealouſy that ſomething was ſcheming between the Engliſh and Ragobah, or that the miniſters were chagrined at not having him in their power, they complained to Colonel Upton, that the Bombay council had not reſtored the places which were to be ceded by treaty; that they had ſupplied Ragobah with military ſtores: adding, that Hyder had purſued proper meaſures in inforcing his treaties by arms; and that if, in theſe particulars, ſatisfaction was not given them they would carry fire and ſword through all the Company's territories. The Bombay council denied theſe aſſertions; they ſaid, that as to the places ceded, they had ſent orders to Surat and Broach to have the pergunnahs delivered up upon the appearance of perſons properly authorized to receive them; that no ſuch had appeared; that remonſtrances had been made to Ragobah, but his inability to pay prevented his diſbanding his forces: that their garriſoning Surat and Broach was an act of neceſſity, no way inconſiſtent with peace, ſince it prevented accidents which might happen from the neighbourhood of the troops of either party; that they were ſo far from plotting to renew the war, that when the Nizam had lately offered his aſſiſtance to Ragobah, if the Engliſh would engage not to take part with the Mahrattas, they had declined giving any ſuch promiſe. They on their ſide complained, that no good effects had yet appeared from the treaty, that to the great detriment of the Engliſh, no communication or intercourſe was yet permitted with the Mahratta dominions; which prohibition was ſo rigid that no perſons were permitted to come from the neighbouring ports to Bombay, even to ſell vegetables or other proviſions; that the Mahratta fleet had taken ſix veſſels coming from Goa under Engliſh colours

lours which had been ſeparated by a ſtorm from their convoy, and carried them into Gheriah; that they had refuſed ſending a Vaqueel to Bombay to explain the reaſon of this behaviour; that it was not poſſible to execute that part of the treaty which related to the country ceded by Futty Sing, he redemanding this from Ragobah, upon this ground, that the conditions of the treaty with him were not performed; that he denied that the Poonah government had any right to demand them, or any thing to do with theſe revenues, all that related thereto having been fully ſettled in the year 1759, when a diviſion was made of the Guzurat country between Poonah and the Gwicawars. Thus each party ſtarted difficulties, and the treaty remained without any article of it being fully carried into execution. A whole year was ſpent in altercations and mutual complaints, when the year 1777 opened a new ſcene.

In the beginning of April a French ſhip arrived at Collaby, a place at the entrance into the river of Choul, which landed ſeveral gentlemen, who ſending notice of their arrival to Poonah, had not only leave given them to go thither, but were received in great pomp, there being an eſcort ordered of twenty-five Arab ſepoys with an elephant, twenty camels, a palanquin, and ſome horſe. The perſon who appeared to be chief among them ſtyled himſelf Chevalier de St. Lubin, a man already well known in the Engliſh ſettlements in India for his intrigues.

This man, on the 17th of April, was received and had long conferences at Porounder. Mr. Moſtyn who now reſided at Poonah, on behalf of the Engliſh remonſtrated againſt his admiſſion to the Durbar, but he was anſwered that his preſent reception was in conſequence of an application made two years and a half before, and that matters had then ſo far advanced, that his reception could not be now refuſed. The ſhip was brought up to Choul, where her loading, conſiſting of artillery, fire-arms, copper, and cloth, was landed. St. Lubin aſſured the Durbar that two ſhips more would ſoon arrive, for which he demanded permiſſion to winter in their harbours. On the 8th of May he had an audience of the Paiſhwa, in which he preſented credentials from the king of France.

It

It was much doubted, not only by the English, but by the French resident in India, whether St. Lubin had any commission of the kind he pretended, or was at all authorized: Monf. Belcombe, commandant at Pondicherry, refused to acknowledge him as ambassador, but the French agent at Surat answered his draughts: the persons who accompanied him suspected him. The truth, from the information of the principal among these who had fallen out with him, and took refuge with Mr. Mostyn the English resident at Poonah, appeared to be, that St. Lubin had jointly with Monf. Dumas, an officer of rank in the Canada army last war, and governor of the Isle of France, obtained Monf. de Sartine's approbation and consent to a plan they had formed, which was, that St. Lubin should embark at Bourdeaux, on board a ship called La Paix, as minister plenipotentiary in the department of commerce to the Mahratta court; Monf. Dumas was to embark at Brest on L'Indien at the head of 1500 men, which were to be joined by 1000 to be shipped on board La Paix, the whole 2500 to be under the command of Dumas, who was to have the department of war in the expedition, as St. Lubin had of

 com-

commerce, and 500 more were to be landed at the Isle of France by a private merchant ship. Mons. de Sartine actually visited the ports where the ships lay. St. Lubin, who wanted to be at the head of all, by his private insinuations prevailed on him (unknown to Dumas, who then thought him gone to Lyons to take leave of his friends) to consent that he should sail in a private ship from Bourdeaux, that he might prepare all things for the reception of the force which was to follow under the command of Dumas; this was to join the Mahrattas, after which they were to strike some great stroke. St. Lubin had the powers of insinuation to a great degree; plausible, assuming, and ready of speech, he gave what he said an air of truth, yet he was superficial, and ever ready to sacrifice truth and every thing to his interest, even to the detriment of his own nation. By his representations of the mighty advantages that would result to France in general, and in particular to those persons who embarked with him, he carried out some gentlemen from Bourdeaux, who soon after their arrival in India, saw they were the dupes of their credulity, and that things at Poonah were in reality very different from what

what he had represented them to be. By the first packet he sent to France, which was to go by Surat, they wrote to their friends what they saw: these letters he opened, and from that time became their enemy; and so violent was his persecution, that he prevailed on Nanah to order one of them, Monf. Corcelle, to be put to death, after having himself attempted to kill him: another person was seized by mistake, and would have been thrown under an elephant's feet, had not a bramin found he was a Dane. The protection granted to this Monf. Corcelle and Mr. Madget by Mr. Lewis, the then English resident, was made a subject of complaint, in the bickerings which followed. For from that time the English resident met with a treatment, which fully shewed the effect of St. Lubin's negotiations and promises.

Nanah Furneze, then the acting person in the Paishwa's ministry, entered into confidence with him on his undertaking to bring a considerable military force to Poonah, completely furnished with artillery and stores; and an alliance was to be concluded between France and the Mahratta nation. That his promises might be effected, Nanah gave him the free uſe of the port of Choul. At this time Saccaram and Nanah were the principal miniſters at Poonah; Saccaram was old and infirm, and reſiding in Porounder, acted moſtly in the care of the perſon of the infant Paiſhwa. Nanah, about the age of fifty, active and enterprizing, aſpired to the chief rule, likely to devolve upon him at the death of Saccaram.

From the protection he had afforded Mr. Bolts before the arrival of St. Lubin, and his connections ſince with that miniſter, it is apparent his diſpoſitions were not favourable to the Engliſh. Another perſon, who might be looked on as a miniſter at Poonah, was Morabah, nephew of Nanah, a man of great influence and ability, and alſo of great prudence; till that time avoiding interference in thoſe troubled ſcenes; inclined to Ragobah.

Sindia and Holcar who hold the country extending from Guzurat to the banks of the Jumma, originally paid a tribute, but in the preſent weakneſs of government are grown independent. A moiety of Guzurat and Salcet, Baſſein, and the country of Broach, belonged

longed to the Paiſhwa family; the Bouncelo family poſſeſs Berar and Nagpoor in perfect ſovereignty.

The intereſt of St. Lubin at Poonah was an alarming circumſtance. It was ſo high with Nanah, that, in order to prevent any opportunity the Engliſh reſident might have of procuring intelligence, he prevailed on him to place guards upon his houſe. This was not the only inſult; on his complaining of this treatment, he was anſwered, that all Europeans ſhould leave Poonah; that if the Engliſh deſired to have an agent there, a Carcoon (that is an inferior perſon) would anſwer the purpoſe, and Nanah expreſsly deſired he would inform the Bombay preſidency of this. This meſſage was highly reſented by them, and a diſavowal of it inſiſted on, but in vain; on the contrary, the reſtraint was increaſed.

Other circumſtances concurred to ſhew that ſome ſchemes againſt the Engliſh were forming. The French agents and chiefs were buſy every where. General Belcombe had a ſixty-four gun ſhip ready, in which he was to be carried to the coaſt of Malabar, with a com-a company of Europeans, a large ſuite, and ſome arms; Mahi was the place named, and it was given out he was only going to viſit that ſettlement; but the real view was to bring to maturity the plans formed between St. Lubin and Nanah; this appeared fully by the proceedings which followed.

The diſſenſions among the miniſters at Poonah were now conſiderable, Mr. Moſtyn, the Engliſh reſident there, had for ſome time perceived the ſeeds of a revolution. On the 10th of December 1777, the council of Bombay received advice that Saccaram, Morabah, Butchaba a man of conſiderable influence, together with Holcar, had confederated to remove Nanah from his employment, and reſtore Ragobah, provided the council of Bombay would join them, and with a military eſcort conduct him to Poonah. That each of theſe chiefs had the command of 10,000 horſe, and that Sindia, who was then abſent at the diſtance of ſixty leagues from Poonah, was ſuppoſed to be in the ſame intereſt. At this time Furkia, the commander of the Mahratta forces for the miniſters, was on the borders of the Carnatic, where he had invaded Hyder Ally, who in in two engagements had totally defeated him. And Raja Ram, the nominal ſovereign of the Mahratta empire, died the beginning of January.

The council of Bombay thought great advantage in the preſent circumſtance might be reaped from this confederacy; but as by the treaty of Porounder Ragobah was totally excluded, it was judged proper that Saccaram, who was the principal actor in that treaty, ſhould, jointly with the other confederates, ſend the propoſal in writing and under ſeal; this done, they promiſed the concurrence deſired. The 12th of December they advertized the Supreme Council of the whole matter. The governor general looked upon this as a favourable opportunity of counteracting the operations of St. Lubin, and therefore propoſed upon thoſe conditions to authorize the Bombay council to conclude ſuch an agreement, and promiſe them aſſiſtance in men and money; the reſolution paſſed, and ten lacks of roupies in bills were immediately forwarded to Bombay; and that council was expreſsly enjoined to adhere to the requiſition that Saccaram and the other perſons ſhould ſend the propoſal under their ſeals and ſignatures,

tures, and by no means to act, unless that condition was complied with. This was done in February 1778.

As it was judged that the council of Bombay were not of strength sufficient singly to carry so great a design into execution, nor to withstand the effect of St. Lubin's intrigues, should they succeed so far as to introduce a French army into the Mahratta state, it was thought prudent to have a force at hand ready to act as occasion should require. The country between the Ganges and Bombay and Poonah was now well known, and no more thought impassable for an army; the governor general therefore proposed to send a detachment under Colonel Leslie, an officer of ability, through the inland country towards Bombay, which might be at hand to act as occasion should require. It consisted of six battalions of sepoys and one company of native artillery, which were to be joined by a regiment of cavalry and a body of horse from the province of Owde; these were all to assemble at Kulpee, near the Jumna, and from thence proceed, through the countries of Boondelchund and Berar, towards Bombay.

On

Colonel Leslie had served in the late war under General Wolfe, and by his zeal and activity had so far recommended himself to the favour of that superior judge of military merit, that he was among the few distinguished friends to whom the general had by his will given honourable tokens of his regard. This reputation he had supported in the course of his service in India, he had particularly distinguished himself in the Rohilla war by a judicious attention and unremitting exertion in the duty of quarter-master-general, though part of the time labouring with the gout. His instructions were, "To proceed by the most practicable route to Bombay, or such other parts as he should be directed to by the committee of that presidency; he was to prefer the route through the Boondelchund country and province of Berar, but if refused by that Rajah, not to persist, but according to his judgment and the result of his enquiries vary his route, making it his first care to reconcile the chiefs to his passage through their countries, but at all events to prosecute his march, from the beginning of which he was to obey such orders from Bombay as were not contrary to the tenor of his instructions. He was advised of the several letters written to the

chiefs,

chiefs, and particularly the Rajah of Berar, to procure passports and supplies of provisions; and it was recommended to him to cultivate a good understanding with them, particularly the latter; he was authorised to use every expedient necessary for the safety and supply of the detachment without infringing the peace subsisting with the Mahratta state, and to adhere to the treaty of Porounder: the strictest order and discipline was recommended, and every attention to preserve any possible imputation of blame, nor was he to act offensively, even at the requisition of the Bombay Council, unless they should declare that there was actually a war, and he was to advertise them as frequently as possible of his progress."

These instructions corresponded with those given to Mr. Alexander Elliot *, who for his talents in negotiation, was unanimously chosen an Ambassador to the Rajah of Berar, with whom the governor general had long kept a correspondence.

* Mr. Elliot was brother to the present Sir Gilbert Elliot, and was a young man of surprizing knowledge, ability, and diligence; unfortunately for the Company and his country, he died before he could execute his commission.

The

The revenues of this Raja amount to one hundred and fifty lacks yearly, and he is at the head of 30,000 horſe.

Modagee, related by blood to the Rajas of Poonah, had been adopted by Sahoo the predeceſſor of Ram Raja, and looked to the ſovereignty of the Mahratta ſtate at the death of Sahoo; but Ballagee, then Paiſhwa, defeated this ſucceſſion, and raiſed Ram to the throne: Ragogee, the father of Modagee, to aſſert his ſon's right, marched with a conſiderable force to Poonah; but the Paiſhwa found means to appeaſe him by conceſſions of great value; the moſt conſiderable was the independence of all the Bouncelo poſſeſſions. In the year 1773 Shabagee, one of the ſons of Ragogee, being then chief of Berar, had ſent a Vaqueel to Calcutta with an offer of alliance. Mr. Haſtings, then preſident of that government, propoſed conditions ſimilar to thoſe which had been granted to Sujah Doulah the Nabob of Owde. Shabagee being ſlain, this negociation dropped, and the change of government at Calcutta, by the forming of the Supreme Council, deſtroyed the probability of renewing it; yet the Vaqueel was by Mr. Haſtings kept ſome time in hopes that

that there yet might offer an opportunity of doing it with effect, but he had lately sent him home. Modagee, when settled, sent him back to Calcutta with a tender of a friendly alliance; and Mr. Hastings, foreseeing that the troubles in the West of India might draw the English to take some part in them, looked on this as a circumstance which might in some event prove a fortunate connection. On the determination of sending Colonel Leslie's detachment, he wrote to Modagee, desiring a passage through his country. The answer was most friendly; he not only consented, but promised to send to the banks of the Nerbuddah a quantity of grain and other necessaries for the English army, and a body of horse to escort them through his territory; and added, that he had written letters to Colonel Leslie to advise him of this. The escort and stores were accordingly sent.

The situation of affairs convinced the governor general more and more of the necessity of having some resource to counterbalance this interest of the French; it could not be doubted but that if matters in Europe proceeded to a war, the flames of it must spread to India, and the nation which found itself

itſelf ſtrongeſt and beſt prepared would ſtrike ſome ſtroke againſt the other. Bombay and the poſſeſſions of the Engliſh in that quarter were the parts moſt liable to an attack; the directors had warned the Supreme Council of this; every circumſtance warranted their conjecture. Theſe conjectures were but too well founded; and fortunately the governor general had ſomething yet ſtronger to decide him. Mr. Elliot, in his return from England to India, had paſſed through Paris, where he had the opportunity of learning the real ſituation of things from perſons thoroughly inſtructed; he was fully informed of thoſe ſteps which inevitably muſt bring on a war. He knew the whole progreſs of them; this he communicated to the governor general, who by this means ſaw his conjectures become a certainty.

This made him turn his thoughts ſtill more ſtrongly to Berar, and he reſolved to make an alliance with the Raja Modagee, at leaſt defenſive; but which might, according to the occaſions furniſhed by events, be improved to an offenſive one. It was for this purpoſe that Mr. Elliot was choſen to go to the Durbar of Modagee; his inſtructions were to the effect following:

He was to form his judgment on the actual ſtate of that government, the intelligence he ſhould receive from the neighbouring ſtates, and particularly the advices from Bombay, and regulate his proceedings accordingly; and as in the ſeveral matters he might treat of, ſome were in their nature ſuch, that what was ſtipulated muſt be permanent, he was not to conclude any articles concerning theſe without having communicated them to and received the approbation of the Supreme Council; but thoſe where the proviſions were only temporary and required immediate deciſion, he might conclude without ſuch reference.

That as the primary intention was a perpetual defenſive alliance, to have mutual intereſts and reciprocal confidence muſt therefore be the ground-work: on theſe principles he ſhould ſtipulate,

1. That a mutual friendſhip ſhould be eſtabliſhed between the two governments;

ments; that the friends of one ſhould be the friends of the other, and the enemies of one the enemies of the other.

2. That a certain number of troops ſhould be kept up within our frontier in the neareſt and moſt convenient ſituation to his dominions; that a monthly ſubſidy proportionable to the expence ſhould be paid by him.—This article was to contain a power to alter the numbers, or even decline or withdraw the whole.

3. That on his part a body of cavalry ſhould be kept up for the ſervice of the government of Bengal, who ſhould not be the native militia accuſtomed to plunder, but regular troops; that the pay of theſe ſhould be only when employed—This article was not to be indiſpenſable.

Such were his inſtructions as to the articles upon matters permanent in their nature; as to others which were temporary and required deciſion and immediate activity, the grounds on which he was to regulate his conduct, were as follow:

The reſidence of St. Lubin at Poonah, and the intereſt he had cultivated with the miniſters, made it likely that ſome ſtroke might be expected from thence, and as the probability was now that war exiſted between the French and Engliſh, Bombay muſt have been the firſt to feel the effects of it. Deſigns yet greater might be in agitation, and an attack upon Bengal from the internal parts of India, with the aſſiſtance of the Mahratta force, was to be apprehended. The Bombay preſidency were authorized to aſſiſt in carrying on the plan communicated to them in December laſt of excluding Nanah from the government, and reſtoring Ragobah; the detachment ſent under the command of Colonel Leſlie was formed to ſecond theſe endeavours; but the undertaking had failed in the principal part; the change among the miniſters was effected, but Ragobah not reſtored. Thus deprived of the reſource hoped for in the friendſhip of Ragobah, and aiming at obſtructing the French intereſt and counteracting their ſchemes, and it being dangerous without the ſupport of a powerful alliance for the detachment to proceed on its firſt deſtination, it muſt have been a moſt deſirable thing to have a mutual

intereſt

interest, and to join our forces with those of Modagee. This was founded on very good reasons; his dominions lie between those of the government of Bengal and the country dependent on the Paishwa, and border on them and the country of the Nizam. There must exist a natural jealousy between his family and the government of Poonah: their animosity had been increased by many reciprocal acts of violence. Modagee had strong pretensions to the succession of the Raja Ram: he had a natural enemy in the Nizam. The situation of all affairs in those parts was therefore in the first place to be learned.

If the council of Bombay had not entered into new engagements with Ragobah or with the party governing at Poonah which clashed with the following instructions, and that a French force was at Poonah, or that Mr. St. Lubin was still there, or that no circumstance offered to contradict what was already known on that head, a direct union with Modagee for carrying on a war against the Mahrattas at Poonah, was to be offered: in all this great discretion must be used; the principal aim being to defeat the French combination, to prevent their receiving as-

 sistance

ſiſtance in their attack upon Bombay, and to eſtabliſh a connection between the Engliſh and the Mahratta ſtate, to inſure their ſupport againſt the French, or any other nation with whom the Engliſh might be at war.

The negotiation therefore was to be ſuſpended until through the information of the Bombay Council, or of Mr. Moſtyn the reſident at Poonah, the nature of their engagements ſhould be fully known; there muſt be an entire conformity to their meaſures; no offenſive plan whatſoever muſt be adopted which could in any manner counteract them; a defenſive one was, and ever to be, the main object.

The Raja of Berar is a ſovereign and independent power. If the French intereſt with the Poonah government was diſſolved, and no hoſtile intention againſt the Company ſubſiſted, the treaty concluded at Porounder with the Paiſhwa Narrein remained in full force; and no engagement contrary to it muſt be entered into: but this treaty was not contradicted by a defenſive alliance with Berar, nor even by an offenſive one which regarded other powers: nor by the precaution of a ſtationary force

force on the frontier. In return, Modagee might expect from the Company to be assisted in asserting his right to the Rajaship, and in recovering the places conquered from his family by the Nizam; the latter being foreign to our purpose therefore nothing was to be concluded on that head unless an absolute necessity of it was apparent; and then the stipulation must have been confined to the places taken by him since the death of Jannogee.

If the Nizam had joined the French or their allies at Poonah, then the terms proposed by Modagee were to be listened to. If the prospect in the succession to the Rajaship was fair and probable, it would be right to treat upon that matter; our end in it would be answered by the exclusion of French influence: the positive advantage on his side intitled us to demand some return; as the full reimbursement of any charges the Company should be put to, the confirmation of all the cessions made to the Bombay council by Ragobah and Futty Sing, and to the Supreme Council of Bengal by the treaty of Poroundcr; in these matters the council of

Bombay muſt guide. No territory on the Bengal ſide of India was deſired.

Notice to be ſent to the council of Bombay and to Colonel Leſlie of what ſhould be concluded.

He was to take ſpecial care that no part ſhould be taken in the diſturbances annoying the Bouncelo family.

Whatever agreements ſhould be entered into, were not to be reſtrained to the perſon of Modagee, but extend to his ſucceſſors.

Theſe inſtructions ſhew the apprehenſion of the danger, and what remedy was conceived to be the moſt efficacious. There was no neceſſity of changing the ſituation of the detachment from the Bengal ſide of the Nerbudda, or altering its deſtination, till the ſtate of affairs was fully known. It was at hand to act according to the meaſures which ſhould be concerted with Modagee. If the firſt ſcheme failed, it was ready for the ſecond; if they both failed, it was near our frontier. When once the news of a war with France ſhould arrive, it muſt decide what meaſures were abſolutely neceſſary. At

all

all events that influence in the Mahratta ſtate was to be deſtroyed; for if once St. Lubin could bring troops and ſtores to Poonah, whatever party he eſpouſed muſt command obedience; and in that caſe Bombay would not be the only object, the province of Owde muſt be the ſcene of ravage, and probably they might extend their views ſo far as to diſpute the poſſeſſion of Bengal *.

Small is the dependence which in thoſe caſes could be had on Bombay. Some other reſource muſt be found: Modagee, by his

* The following incident ſhews how juſt were theſe apprehenſions. Mr. Elliot in his journey overtook Monſ. Chevalier, chief of Chandernagore, at Cuttack on his way to Poonah, and prevailed on the Naib to aſſiſt in ſeizing him. Among his papers was found a letter from General Belcombe, dated Pondicherry, 12 July 1778, relating to the ſituation of affairs between the Engliſh and French nations, to which was this remarkable poſtſcript:

" It would be proper for me to apprize the Mahrattas " at Cuttack and Berar of the diſpoſition of the Engliſh " reſpecting a war, which appears to be inevitable; and " that I ſhould write to thoſe at Poonah, that this is the " moment to unite, in order to cruſh that ambitious na- " tion, who hath already met with conſiderable loſſes in " America, which they ſeek to repair by ſubjecting all the " princes of India."

Other letters intercepted by the Bombay council ſhewed the reality of the French deſigns, and how much they at that time exerted their whole powers to bring them to maturity.

ſituation,

ſituation, by his intereſts, and by his inclinations, was the moſt probable one.

The advantages ariſing from this ſcheme muſt be great. A body of troops kept on our frontier in the manner propoſed, increaſes our force without any expence to us. The Berar cavalry is the beſt in India: the ſtation of the troops muſt cauſe a concourſe of people in thoſe parts, which may bring into cultivation that region, now neglected, though the ſoil is good and capable of fertility. An inland communication with Bombay and Madras will be opened, and a barrier will be formed on that ſide of our poſſeſſions.

But a yet greater advantage follows this ſtation: Nangpoor * is the center of the peninſula; the army may thence conveniently reach the dominions of the ſurrounding princes, and act either for their defence or to their annoyance. They muſt behold our power and the poſſeſſions ceded to us with jealouſy, which our European enemy is watchful to improve. The loſs of the northern circars muſt affect the Nizam; he was then in league with the French and the Poo-

* The capital of Berar.

nah miniſtry; his brother Bazalet Jung, who had for his life the poſſeſſion of the circar of Gontour, between the territory of the Nabob of Arcot and that of Mazulipatam, had at this hour five hundred French in his ſervice, which all the repreſentations and endeavours of the council of Madras had proved ineffectual to remove from that country. No emplacement of our troops could be ſo formidable to thoſe princes as that near Berar. The bare inſpection of the map of India ſhews the importance of the ſituation of that province in regard to the three great powers who bound our poſſeſſions. The prince of Berar is our natural ally; he hath no intercourſe with France: the firſt ſtep of the Poonah alliance muſt have been an invaſion of his territory to force him to lend his aſſiſtance to their attack of Bengal.

The trade of this province is another very material article: it produces the beſt cotton in India, which is ſpun into fine thread, and exported in that ſtate to the dominions of the Company. The duties are at preſent high; but even under this diſadvantage theſe manufactures yield the greateſt profit of any brought from India. The Dutch, beſides ſpices, ſend great

great quantities of copper into Berar; this article may be turned in our favour. The climate ſome months in the year is comparatively cold; this may produce a demand for woollens. Many other advantages there may be which commerce itſelf will bring forth.

Another revolution in the Poonah miniſtry demonſtrated the aſcendency of French influence. On the 25th of Auguſt letters were received at Calcutta from Bombay, mentioning that Nanah had recovered his rank and influence, upon which Morabah had applied to them for immediate aſſiſtance to conduct Ragobah to Poonah, ſending articles ſubſcribed by him and Butchabah; Holcar agreeing to this by a ſeparate paper under his hand, that they approved of the propoſal, but had deferred acting in conſequence to the month of September, that they might in the mean time be authorized by the Supreme Council, or receive directions from London. The anſwer authorized them to proceed, provided what they ſhould undertake did not endanger their ſafety, or prove contrary to any engagements which Mr. Elliot might have entered into with Modagee. This anſwer was tranſmitted through him, who was

at

at the ſame time to let them know the ſtate of the negotiation. Thus by the mutual correſpondence which muſt ariſe from the obſervation of his inſtructions with regard to that preſidency, it was probable that on either ſide nothing could be done but what was beſt adapted to the ſtate of affairs in the Weſt of India.

Before the detachment marched the governor general, to prevent any danger which might happen by Bengal being left open to a French invaſion, had taken the following precautions: a naval force was prepared; two ſhips of forty guns each had already joined Sir Edward Vernon, and there remained in the mouth of the Ganges two frigates and three cruiſers, under the command of an excellent officer *, which, joined to what was already in that region, muſt keep off any armament of our enemies, and cleanſe that ſea from pirates which annually infeſt it: and a ſupply of troops in the room of that detachment was provided. The army was augmented with nine battalions of ſepoys: the companies had before been augmented to eighty rank and file: theſe might upon oc-

* Captain John Richardſon who had ſerved with credit in the late war.

caſion

cafion be formed into four battalions of feven hundred men each. The artillery was augmented with two companies of Europeans, and four battalions of native artillery-men; thefe, with fome addition, are compofed of Lafcars, who have now the advantage of difcipline given to their former laborious duties; befides this, the militia, amounting to one thoufand men, was embodied. This, with the alliance at Berar, muft fufficiently fecure Bengal by land: and there is no probability of fuccefs to an invafion of it by fea; for the inconveniencies are too many and too confiderable: the feafon of fetting out; the feafon of arrival; the number of troops neceffary; the quantity of ftores and ammunition of all kinds; the number of fhips of war and tranfports; the length of fuch an embarraffed voyage; the chance of lofs by fickncfs and death; on the landing the want of cattle, artificers, and coolies; all thefe militate againft fuch an undertaking. The true way of invading Bengal is through the provinces, by alliances with the powers of the country; the Mahrattas are the only power to ferve this purpofe, and a firm eftablifhed friendfhip with Berar the moft effectualy way of preventing the effects of fuch an alliance. On the other hand, every thing calls

calls them to Bombay, the neighbourhood of the Mahrattas, and the convenience of the port of Choul, are advantages not to be met with in other parts of India.

Whilst these things passed in Calcutta, the proceedings at Bombay were, by the fluctuations at Poonah, rendered variable, and could not answer the warmth with which they at first set out. On the 19th of January 1778, they received advice that an agreement had been signed at Poonah between the ministers and St. Lubin, by which the French were to have Row Dunda or Choul, that they might the better carry in their troops and artillery. Upon this they resolved that nothing but a change in the administration at Poonah could secure the Company from the dangers and bad consequences of the alliance between the French and Mahrattas; and that there was no method of averting the evil impending, but by the Company taking a decisive part. They communicated this to the Supreme Council, who approved it; and recommended to them to obtain the following conditions:

1. The personal safety of Ragobah.

2. That

2. That a ſpecific ſum be ſtipulated for the military charges incurred by this interpoſition.

3. That Baſſein and its diſtrict be ceded in perpetuity to the Company.

4. An additional grant of territory adjacent to Baſſein and Bombay, in exchange for Broach, the lands ceded by Futty Sing, and the Pergunnahs of Hanſood, Aſhmood, and Derborah.

5. That no European ſettlement ſhall be allowed in the Mahratta dominions, without the conſent of the Supreme Council; but this to be only extended to the enemies of Britain.

6. That a ſupply of ten lacks of roupies be immediately granted to the preſidency of Bombay for the ſupport of their engagements.

And at the ſame time, that they might be prepared for all events, requeſted the preſidency of Madras to have two hundred Europeans, half a company of artillery, and a battalion of ſepoys

ſepoys ready to march to Anjengo, thence to be tranſported to Bombay, if required.

Saccaram was backward in putting his name to this inſtrument, though he acted privately with the confederates. Morabah would have taken the whole upon himſelf, and engaged, that if the Engliſh and he underſtood each other, he would ſettle the government in a month's time; but the Board inſiſted; and this kept back the concluſion of a treaty between them.

The diſpoſitions of the ſeveral powers of the Mahrattas and their armies in January 1778, were as follows: Modagee Bouncelo was at Lacanwady Gaut, thirty coſs eaſtward of Aurengabad; Holcar was at his own village Banbgam, with 12,000 horſe, and five or ſix thouſand Praeds *, refuſing any correſpondence with Nanah. Sindia endeavouring to raiſe contributions on Janogee Patancars jaghire, near Rimetpore, had occaſioned a ſkirmiſh, in which Janogee was killed. Furkia had been again defeated by Hyder, and retreated to Panchmach, a place belonging to the Nizam, on the north bank of the Kriſtna, in hopes of receiving aſſiſtance from

* Foot ſoldiers and ſlingers.

Downſa, one of Nizam's generals, who was encamped about twelve coſs from him. Hyder Ally, in purſuit of him had croſſed to the north of Jongebodra. The Nizam, though ſtrongly ſolicited to join the Poonah force againſt him, refuſed, unleſs the forts of Aſhur and Armadanagur, formerly promiſed, were delivered to him. Furkia was ſoon after yet more unfortunate; for Badgee Punt Burwa, joined by ſeveral other Mahratta chiefs, attacked and routed his army, taking three elephants, his cannon, and plundering his Buzar *, he eſcaping only with five hundred horſe. Theſe different events, and particularly the laſt, were fatal to Nanah: his reſource was to go to Porounder, in hopes, by the means of Saccaram, to perſuade Sindia to go to the aſſiſtance of Furkia; who, far from receiving aſſiſtance from Downſa, had been by him deſired to remove, from Panchmach, and had retreated to Serapore twenty coſs north of Kriſtna: his ſcattered army there joined him, and he ſoon again approached to Downſa, ſtill retaining hopes of aſſiſtance, notwithſtanding his inclinations muſt have been againſt him, as he had a daughter contracted to Tippoo Sahed the ſon

* Buzar or Bazar, a market.

of

of Hyder *. But theſe hopes were kept up by his knowing that a Vaqueel from the Nizam had been ſent to Poonah. The reſult of Nanah's conference with Saccaram was a reſolution to endeavour by all means to procure the aſſiſtance of Holcar and Sindia to Furkia, and to ſend him money and 3000 men. Shortly after, in the month of March, he was again ſurprized, and his whole force was reduced to 3000, with whom he retreated along the Kriſtna towards Meritz.

Thus the whole of the Mahratta ſtate was a ſcene of confuſion: each chief ſolely intent upon his private concerns, watching to advance his own intereſts as occaſion ſhould offer, and all in continual diſtruſt of each other. Through all this chaos the party againſt Nanah continued their ſcheme of changing the government, and their intercourſe with Mr. Moſtyn; but Saccaram ſtill delayed his ſignature to the requeſt of aſſiſtance from Bombay. At laſt Mr. Moſtyn was aſſured by the confederates, that on the

* Whether this alliance or other cauſes made him the object of the Nizam's ſupicions, he was within a ſhort time after taken off.

22d of March Morabah, Butchaba, and Holcar would move, that in five or six days they would appear on Porounder plain with 25,000 men; that Saccaram waited for that event fully to declare himself, and would give Mr. Moſtyn entire ſatisfaction; that they ſhould ſeize and impriſon Nanah; that Morabah would write to the preſident, and alſo to Ragobah, which letters ſhould be accompanied with the Bul Bundar, which is an oath of fidelity; that Holcar would alſo write to Ragobah.

On the 26th about noon Morabah and ſome other chiefs encamped on the oppoſite ſide of the river with 10,000 horſe. A detachment of fifty horſe entered Poonah, twenty-five of which marched to the palace, the others patrolled the ſtreets, directing the inhabitants in Ragobah's name, to keep quietly to their occupations, and promiſing ſafety for perſon and effects to thoſe who ſhould do ſo. An hour after Morabah arrived and went directly to the palace, where, paying his reſpects to Perwetty Bah *, he received from her

* Perwetty Bah was the wife of Subadah, who had been confined with the widow of Naron in the fort of Porounder,

her the ſirpaw of Duan *, he began by placing his own people in the room of thoſe who were the guard, whom he diſmiſſed: the houſe of the Duan who had been appointed by Nanah had ſome of thoſe new guards placed upon it. He then publickly received the compliments due to his ſtation, after which he returned to his tents on the other ſide of the river, where he was to meet Holcar, who had advanced to the diſtance of three coſs; Saccaram lay diſtant about ſix coſs. They were all to join in the morning, when their whole force would amount to 30,000, and march to Porounder, whence they were to ſend a perſon of conſequence to Bombay, who ſhould attend Ragobah to Poonah. On the 30th of March an agent arrived at Bombay, ſent by them, who in their name deſired that no time ſhould be loſt in ſending Ragobah to Poonah; but no particular propoſals were mentioned. The Bombay council, in ſo turbid an appearance, could not determine what direction to give miniſter at Poonah; they left his conduct there

rounder, and after the death of Naron's widow, had the care of the infant Paiſhwa. It is not eaſy to conceive how ſhe came to be ſo intruſted.

* Duan is treaſurer, and principal miniſter.

to his own discretion, and his regard for the interests of the Company: but at the same time that they might be ready to profit by any events favorable, and which led to decision, they determined to prepare three hundred English infantry, two companies of artillery lascars, with a suitable field train. Colonel Egerton was to command this body, next in command to him was Colonel Cockburn.

The aspect of affairs at Poonah now promised the establishment of Ragobah. On the 28th of March Nanah was at the foot of the hill of Porounder with 5000 men. All his endeavours to encrease this force were vain; he was therefore compelled to submit to accept conditions from the party of Saccaram and Morabah; he agreed to accept an inferior office. Saccaram and Morabah were to be guarantees for his life and treasures. In this agreement no mention was made of Ragobah. The effect of this union was that Nanah's political system gained ground: Mr. Mostyn found that Morabah was not willing to abandon Bassein; and he wrote to the council, that Ragobah must not depend on a force to receive him there, that it could

be

be had only from Bombay, and ſhould conſiſt of at leaſt two battalions, with a ſuitable train of artillery.

Ragobah, on the other hand, giving full ſcope to his hopes, and ſhutting his eyes to all difficulties, was extremely preſſing for his departure. The council remonſtrated againſt this impatience, inſiſting that it was not proper to move, until a regular invitation, ſuch as had at firſt been promiſed, ſhould have come from Poonah. To this he anſwered, that his appearance would bring matters to a concluſion; that for want of it his partiſans would imagine that the Engliſh were backward in his cauſe, which muſt diſpirit them, and might tempt them to make terms with his enemies; that this was a criſis not to be neglected; that, added to ſome force which he had at Culwa oppoſite Tanna, the troops that could be furniſhed from Bombay were fully ſufficient to complete his re-eſtabliſhment. He aſſented to confirm the treaty of Surat, and expreſſed his wiſhes to enter into an alliance offenſive and defenſive, which ſhould be bound by the ſtrongeſt ties: he promiſed to grant Pergunnahs contiguous to Bombay, for a ſecurity of payment of the troops. At the ſame time he deſired that the Britiſh commander ſhould have orders from the council not to intermeddle with his government; and he intimated that all the grants of territory yielded by his enemies to the Nizam and other powers ſhould be reſumed.

The Mahratta chiefs ſtill continued in their encampments. Mr. Moſtyn, on the 10th of April was requeſted by a particular letter from the Durbar, ſealed with the great ſeal, to go to that near Currich, where he was met by Morabah, who told him that Gopal Naique Tumbackar (who was the brother of Butchaba) was to be ſent immediately to Poonah, and requeſted him to meet them at Nanah's camp near Porounder hill, where they were then going He acquieſced, and was received with due ceremony, and marks of regard in a public tent, and introduced to the Durbar, where were preſent Saccaram, Morabah, Nanah, Butchaba, and ſeveral other chiefs, particularly Gopal Naigue Tumbacker. Great civilities were ſhewn him; but a final ſettlement with the Company was put off to Ragobah's arrival. Saccaram requeſted that Mr. Moſtyn would accompany the

the perſon they were to ſend to Bombay; and upon his enquiring into the ſtate of the French alliance, he was anſwered, that they had then under conſideration the immediate diſmiſſion of St. Lubin. The next day Tumbacker told him that on the morrow he was to ſet out; that a Durbar would be held for that purpoſe; that after calling at Poonah, he would proceed to Tanna. On the 16th Mr. Moſtyn had another conference with the chiefs, who requeſted that he would aſſure Ragobah of their good intentions, and that they intreated him not to be induced by any reports to believe the contrary. Mr. Moſtyn then took leave of Morabah. Notwithſtanding thoſe fair appearances things were far from being in a proſperous way: unaccountable remoras to Tumbackers journey appeared from day to day upon frivolous pretences, the principal of which were that ſome particular ſtipulations were to be made with Rogobah, and ſome objections that he made to the perſon of Tumbacker, whom he expreſsly deſired not to be ſent on this deputation to him, were to be anſwered and got over. Neither did matters go on ſmoothly at Bombay: that council had received notice from Bengal of the intended march of the detachment,

ment, and of Mr. Elliot's embaſſy. The majority of them conceived that things at Poonah wore ſo favourable an aſpect, that with their own force, without any aſſiſtance, they would be able to bring matters to a favourable concluſion; and therefore that there was no occaſion for the Bengal detachment. Upon this they reſolved to write to the commander not to proceed in his march, but remain with his detachment at Culpee. The reaſons they gave were, that the difficulties to be encountered in the country which lay between Culpee and Bombay were unſurmountable, and therefore the march impracticable, and expoſing the Company's troops without neceſſity: that it was not poſſible to procure for them either paſſes or proviſions; that the apprehenſions expreſſed by the Supreme Council of a war with France, and of attacks upon Bombay were not grounded; and therefore the expence occaſioned by ſuch an undertaking was not warrantable. Meſſ. Draper and Stackhouſe diſſented from this reſolution; they were of opinion the ſituation of the preſidency was not altered either in reſpect of the French or the Mahrattas; that it was well known the French had deſigns againſt Choul. The event has ſhewn how ill-

ill-founded was the reaſoning of the majority on every point. Perhaps there were other motives which occaſioned this reſolve. The detachment, had it reached Bombay, would have had the honour of all the advantages which were inſured by the junction of the forces: this has ſo often influenced chiefs and commanders in all ages, that attributing it to the majority of this council cannot be judging harſhly. Notwithſtanding the oppoſition of Mr. Draper and Mr. Stackhouſe, on the 22d of April, the council wrote to the commander of the detachment, deſiring he would ſtop at Culpee, and not proceed till he ſhould hear further from them. Ragobah's impatience, which daily increaſed, made him look over all difficulties; he preſſed more and more the departure of the troops, and his own: he repeated the detail of advantages that would immediately follow the open and avowed declaration of the Engliſh, that they ſupported his cauſe. He deſired to direct his march by Callian, where he affirmed that Viſiagee Punt, a conſiderable chief, was upon his appearance ready to declare for him, and join his ſtandard. He offered to put the Company into the immediate poſſeſſion of Baſſein, and deſired a ſtate of his account,

account, and the produce of the Pergunnahs to be aſſigned to the Company for the payment of their troops. But his affairs at Poonah were far from the ſituation the apparent zeal of Morabah and Saccaram had repreſented.

The Poonah Durbar were very uneaſy at the march of the detachment from Bengal. The reaſon given for it to them both from the Supreme Council and Bombay, having been the danger that muſt accrue to the Engliſh ſettlement from the French being in poſſeſſion of Choul, they deſired to know if St. Lubin's immediate diſmiſſion would ſatisfy the council, ſo far as to induce them to ſtop its march; they made excuſes for his having been permitted to remain there ſo long; allowing that ſome promiſes had been made, they aſſerted that it was done only with a deſign to amuſe him; they repeated their former reaſons for the delay of Tumbacker; but, upon the whole, they evaded granting the duſtucks or paſſports for facilitating that march through the Mahratta territories.

The Bombay council on the 15th of May ſent their orders to Mr. Moſtyn to ſpeak peremptorily

remptorily to the Poonah Durbar, that they ſhould declare whether they conſidered the treaty of Porounder as ſubſiſting, and the Mahratta ſtate to be bound by it; to demand, agreeably to that treaty, the poſſeſſion of a country producing three lacks near Broach; to inſiſt upon the countries ceded by Futty Sing as they had not produced the proofs required by the treaty; to demand an explicit declaration concerning their engagements with the French; and to require an anſwer in fourteen days; telling them poſitively that a further delay or evaſion would be conſtrued into a refuſal, and that the council ſhould act in conſequence.

At the ſame time they took off the reſtraint they had laid on the march of the detachment, and directed the commander to advance toward the coaſt. The reaſon they gave for their change of opinion was the continuation of the French reſident at Poonah *, and the apparent bad diſpoſition of the Durbar to the Engliſh.

Morabah

* Advices were received at Bombay that General Belcombe, commander at Pondicherry, had come to Mahé in a ſixty gun ſhip; the council judging this to be the effect of

Morabah had a meeting with St. Lubin, at which he told him that the Engliſh jealouſy made it neceſſary, he ſhould abſent himſelf for a time, but it ſhould not alter the friendſhip of the Mahratta nation to the French.

St. Lubin had undertaken to Morabah to bring to Poonah 2000 Europeans within fifteen months, or at leaſt before the detachment from Calcutta could arrive at its deſtination. The Poonah Durbar wrote at the ſame time to the Supreme Council to deſire they would recal the detachment, upon this ground, that they were complying with the

of St. Lubin's intrigues, and fearing the conſequences requeſted Sir Edward Vernon to defer his departure, who promiſed to employ his frigates in ſearching the whole coaſt, but added that he could not loſe any time, but muſt proceed to Madras. General Belcombe's deſtination was ſaid to be Surat, where he was to ſtay during the rains; he did arrive at Tillichery on the 3d of April 1778, in the Brilliant, a ſhip of ſixty-four guns, and brought three hundred Europeans, who landed at Mahé. He got poſſeſſion of a ſmall fort by the ceſſion of the prince of Cherrica, who had orders for that purpoſe from Hyder Ally, whoſe vaſſal he was. This poſſeſſion was of conſequence, as it commanded the approaches to Fort St. George upon Green Hill which is the key to Mahé. Monſ. Bellcombe was to leave Mahé the 26th of April, and return to Pondicherry. It was affirmed the Brilliant brought two hundred ſoldiers from Mangabore.

treaty

treaty of Porounder, that they sincerely intended bringing Ragobah to Poonah; that it was delayed only as it was necessary that Furkia, who was advancing with a large force, should be consulted; that Mons. St. Lubin was dispatched; that his ship had brought nothing but merchandize: and that they meant in all things peace and amity with the English.

In truth Morabah had urged St. Lubin to depart, that he might sooner bring the troops promised, but he still remained at Poonah, saying he would send letters which would bring them as soon as he could do, if he in person went for them. The Durbar at the same time wrote to Modagee Bouncelo, desiring that he would, if possible, by fair means persuade the commander of the detachment to return, and if he could not succeed by fair means to do it by force.

St. Lubin had, in the month of March preceding, written to the captain general at Goa for leave for two French regiments to pass through the Portugueze territories, and to the governor of Damaun for a permission for the French to use that port; both these requests

requests were with great civility refused, as they might tend to a misunderstanding between the two crowns of Great Britain and Portugal, who were in strict alliance and friendship; but liberty was granted for their ships to refresh in the Portugueze harbours, for which purpose they should be allowed fifteen days. St. Lubin in answer endeavoured to reconcile him to his request, and added, that though to yield to the English jealousy, he was obliged to leave Poonah, he should not do so without having fully effected his business.

It was evident that the Durbar were seeking delays, that the rains might come on before any thing was concluded. If they could retard the march of the detachment until that time, they reckoned the rains would then stop their progress, and during that interval the force might arrive which had been promised by St. Lubin, who, notwithstanding the promise of Morabah, remained at Poonah. Hence fresh occasions of delays were found on each application of Mr. Mostyn for the dustucks or passports. At last, he seeing that the dissensions in the Durbar still continued, and that Sindia and Holcar insisted on Ragobah's being brought to Poonah, applied

plied to them separately, and they readily granted him every order he desired for the safe and undisturbed passage of the detachment through their respective dominions.

The presidency of Madras, in consequence of letters from the governor and Supreme Council, had determined to send to Bombay the aid they had requested: they received letters dated the 29th of April, with advice of this: and now once more varied their orders for the route of the detachment, directing their march to Surat.

An attempt was made, about this time, by a relation of the infant Paishwa, who was one of his attendants, to steal his person from the fort; he had carried the child half way down the hill before he was discovered; there being stopped, he was sent to prison, and the child was carried back into the fort.

On the 12th of June the Bombay council received notice from Mr. Baldwin at Grand Cairo of the situation of affairs between the English and French nations, and the state of war they were in.

The uncertainties at Poonah ſtill continued. Nanah, leaving his retreat had gone to Sindia, who received him, and promiſed him ſupport. They ſent to all the officers, requiring their acknowledgment of them as the miniſters of the Paiſhwa.

Ragobah now informed the council that both parties had applied to him, and that even without the appearance of an Engliſh force he might proceed to Poonah, ſure of ſucceſs there. He allowed that both were his enemies; but ſaid their diſcord was ſo great that nothing could go on, which drove them to this application; and he undertook, that his march would not be attended with any oppoſition, eſpecially if the Engliſh force appeared with him, and that the carrying the cannon through the Gauts, and a ſupply of proviſion ſhould be his care.

On the other hand Morabah was retreating from Poonah, having delivered the ſeals and the enſigns of office to Holcar, who ſent them to Sindia, by whom they were delivered to Nanah, whereby he was once more eſtabliſhed in the Durbar; but a very conſiderable number of adherents remained to Morabah,

Morabah, and it was probable, that this conteſt would not end without ſlaughter. Nanah's force in a manner ſurrounding Poonah and Porounder fort, and occupying all the paſſages in the mountains. He treated with Holcar as well as Sindia, and offered each of them immenſe ſums if they would eſpouſe his cauſe.

Nanah and Morabah each now wiſhed interviews with Mr. Moſtyn, who could not form a judgment which of them would ultimately get the better. He had procured a copy of the paper delivered by Nanah to St. Lubin on the 13th of May 1778, expreſsly requiring the aſſiſtance of France, "to puniſh a nation who had raiſed up an "inſolent head, and whoſe meaſure of in-"juſtice was full;" and in reward of this aid promiſing a jaghire to be granted from the circar of the Paiſhwa. About the ſame time the Durbar had ſent an anſwer to Mr. Moſtyn's repreſentations, no way favourable, but inſiſting, that they had in every ſenſe complied with the treaty of Porounder. The council, on the 24th of June, reſolved to have every thing in readineſs to land their forces to accompany Ragobah, whenever it ſhould appear that the paſſes in the mountains were free.

Mr. Moſtyn being returned to Bombay, and having given the ſelect committee there all his information, and remarks on the preceding facts and diſpoſition of affairs, the nature of the country through which the troops muſt march in caſe of their joining Ragobah in his march to Poonah, which he repreſented as very practicable to infantry; the committee, on the 21ſt of July 1778, reſolved unanimouſly, that the Durbar's anſwers were a violation of the treaty of Porounder. That the ſituation of affairs in Europe, and the reſtoration of Nanah Furneze, created a neceſſity of immediate meaſures to effect the ſubverſion of that party which was connected with the French in ſchemes hoſtile to the Company, and for eſtabliſhing at Poonah an adminiſtration with whom a ſecure and permanent alliance could be maintained. That for that end Ragobah muſt be placed in the regency, with a proviſo that the government and Sicca * be continued in the name of the Paiſhwa during his

* The ſcal.

minority, and ſhould be ſurrendered to him at his legal age; that Morabah ſhould be acquainted that they will heartily join in this plan; that an order ſhould now be ſent to the commander of the detachment to purſue the moſt eligible route to Junier or Zener *, avoiding in his march the proximity of Aurengábad, or any part of the Nizam's dominions.

On the 11th of July Morabah had been ſeized by 2000 men of Sindia's force, and kept in the camp; at the ſame time all who were known to eſpouſe his cauſe were ſeized likewiſe, among whom were Viſagu Pont Binny, and Butchaba. Nanah had the name of miniſter, but Sindia had in reality the whole power; Saccaram was not ſo much as conſulted, and it was probable that both he and Nanah would be ſoon confined, and Sindia act openly alone. Soon after both Morabah and Butchaba were confined in different forts. Mr. Lewis the reſident at Poonah, by the renewal of the obſtacles to his correſpondence, ſoon found the influence of Nanah's government. That party now acted as if

* So called in Jeffries's map.

the continuance of their power was ſecure, the armies of Sindia and Furkia each day decreaſed, by their diſcharging numbers of their horſe.

The governor general and Supreme council in the beginning of this month took poſſeſſion of Chandernagore, and wrote to the preſidency of Madras to order a ſufficient corps of troops to be in readineſs to march to Pondicherry, affirming that the war was now certain, and that if they had not received advices or orders to the contrary from England, they ſhould proceed to hoſtilities; beginning by the attack of that place which would be their firſt, as the ſettlement of Mahi or Mahé ſhould be their ſecond capture.

Freſh propoſals came now from Nanah and that party to Ragobah, all which he rejected, and inſiſted upon either being regent, and having the cuſtody of the infant Paiſhwa, or a partition in equal parts of the poſſeſſions of the Paiſhwa family, whereof one ſhare ſhould be his. On the 16th of Auguſt the preſident acquainted the committee, that on this refuſal the meſſenger from Nanah had

had applied to him; but this application being verbal no further notice was taken of it. Sindia, after telling Saccaram, that his age prevented his being uſeful, had ordered him to his houſe, and no more to intermeddle, and had placed a guard on him.

Hyder Ally had now taken Darwar, and was marching towards Merits in order to attack it, on which the Durbar ordered a force to oppoſe him. Beſides this misfortune, they were embarraſſed by the diſobedience of particular chiefs; Nanah had ſent orders to the Killidar of Amdanagur that he ſhould deliver his fort to Sindia, the Killidar replied, he held it for Ragobah; and not only refuſed to ſurrender it, but ſeized three lacks of roupies which belonged to Nanah, and were returning from Aurengabad, where they had been ſecured for him during the late troubles.

St. Lubin had been diſmiſſed by Nanah, but remained at Damaum, and a continual correſpondence was kept up between him and Monſ. Briancourt the French reſident at Surat, upon their ſcheme of procuring troops to arrive at Choul, and thence proceed to

 Poonah;

Poonah; and by intercepted correſpondence with Pondicherry, it appeared that Nanah had not only required the aid of France as abovementioned, but that it was ſtipulated that the French ſhould, as ſoon as it was practicable, move againſt the Engliſh, for which firſt ſervice they ſhould receive twenty lacks of roupies, and ten ſhips with ſepoys; and upon their attacking Bombay they ſhould receive twenty lacks more: by one of thoſe letters, on pretence of the war being begun, they demanded payment of the firſt twenty lacks.

It was now the 12th of October, when Mr. Carnac delivered a minute to the Bombay council, repreſenting that much time had paſſed ſince the 21ſt of July, on which day they had reſolved to aſſiſt Ragobah, the inconveniencies of a delay, and the advantages which might be taken of the preſent ſituation of the Poonah Durbar diſtracted by diviſions, and their army not yet aſſembled: this was ſeconded by the information and opinion of Mr. Moſtyn, who added, that the adherents to Morabah muſt conclude, if this opportunity was ſuffered to ſlip, that Ragobah was given up. He further ſaid, as to the diſtance at which the detachment ſtill was, that though

it

it might have been of more material advantage if nearer; yet even in its then present situation, which was near Sindia's capital, it would be of great use by keeping him in awe, and thus facilitate their enterprize, whilst on their side, that enterprize by fixing the attention of the Durbar, would prevent the obstacles which might otherwise annoy and retard the march; and he added, that the longer the execution of the resolve was delayed, the greater the French influence, and the more effectual the preparations at Poonah would prove; on which it was resolved by the majority (Mr. Draper dissenting) that the resolution of the 21st of July for conducting Ragobah to Poonah be forthwith carried into execution; and Mr. Lewis was directed to hold himself ready to leave Poonah at a moment's warning.

On the 3d of November the resident and whole French factory at Surat were made prisoners of war by orders from Bombay. They continued some time at Surat confined to their garden, being permitted to remain there to prevent inconvenience in their private arrangements; but it was soon found that intrigues were carrying on for the delivery

very of the caſtle of Surat to the Mahrattas, in which they had a conſiderable ſhare; they were then transferred to Bombay.

At this time news was received there that Pondicherry had, on the 18th of October, ſurrendered to the Engliſh, by which event the government of Madras were enabled to ſend a detachment to reduce the French ſettlement at Mahé. This reduction was ſoon after completed.

On the 4th of November the council, to carry their plan into execution, appointed a committee, conſiſting of Mr. Carnac, Colonel Egerton, and Mr. Moſtyn, which was called the Poonah committee; it was to make the arrangements proper for that ſervice, to communicate the intentions of the Board to Ragobah, and finally to ſettle with him the previous conditions on which the aſſiſtance was given. Colonel Egerton, who, at the time of appointment, did not ſuppoſe they were to accompany him in that capacity on the intended expedition, and therefore had approved the meaſure, now proteſted againſt it, as being contrary to the orders of the Directors, and as unneceſſary, inaſmuch as no negotiation

negotiation could take place on the road, upon which the orders of the ſelect committee could not be had in a ſhort time, and as the orders of the Directors were, that in the abſence of the commander, the ſelect committee ſhould conſiſt of the governor, and ſecond and fourth in council, the abſence of Mr. Carnac who was ſecond, would prove a direct breach of thoſe orders. Mr. Draper on this laſt ground adhered to him, but it was carried by the governor's caſting vote, that two would be a ſufficient ſelect committee, and the meaſure paſſed.

Things were again retarded by a difference with Ragobah. A circular letter was prepared to be iſſued by him on his landing on the continent, in which, aſſuming no higher titles than thoſe uſed by Badgerow in the treaty of 1739, he declared that his view was only to take the adminiſtration out of improper hands, and exerciſe the regency during the minority of the young Paiſhwa, in which he would conduct affairs, and continue the Sicca in the Paiſhwa's name. This letter being ſhewn to him he objected to thoſe clauſes, but afterward ſeemed to acquieſce, on condition the council would lend him the further ſum of three

lacks

lacks of roupies, and furniſh ſome military ſtores; but the letter being left with him, he made alterations therein, whereby it differed widely from the intent propoſed; aſſuming in the title a name of dignity which belongs only to a Paiſhwa, and totally omitting the clauſes relating to the adminiſtration and Sicca. It was reſolved, that if he did not acquieſce in the form preſented to him, and accede to the propoſed conditions, the buſineſs ſhould proceed no further.

After ſome conſideration he conſented to the terms propoſed in the letter, withal deſiring that it might be repreſented to the Company, that he inſiſted that child was ſuppoſitious, and that in caſe he could prove it he ſhould be at liberty to aſſume the Paiſhwaſhip; if he could not, that a partition might be made of the country, and its government, agreeable to the law of the Gentoos.

Three lacks of roupies were now advanced, and 1500 muſkets and five field pieces granted to him, the committee repreſenting that as the Engliſh troops would have more than ſufficient, a greater number would be an incumbrance.

The

The body ordered for the ſervice conſiſted of 143 artillery, with 500 Laſcars, 448 rank and file European infantry, and 2278 ſepoys, making in the whole, officers included, 3900 men.

The treaty ſettled with Ragobah was to the effect of the abovementioned conditions; and by the laſt article the treaty of Surat was in every point confirmed, and the following places aſcertained as the poſſeſſions of the Company:

Baſſein fort and town with its diſtricts and full dependencies: Jamboſieir and Orpad, and the iſland of Canary; an aſſignment upon the Pergunnah of Occlaſier for 75,000 roupies a year: all the ſmall places belonging to the diſtrict of Salcet, which were to be reſtored; and the Pergunnahs of Aſhmood and Hanſood; regular ſunnuds were to be iſſued under the Paiſhwa's Sicca for the abſolute free grant of all theſe places; beſides,

He engaged to pay for the 4000 men with which he was to be aſſiſted, two lacks and a half of roupies a month. No European ſettlements were to be allowed in the Mahratta

Mahratta dominions, without the consent of the Company or their representatives. And it was agreed that if any article of this treaty interfered with any engagements which might have been taken by the Supreme Council, it should be liable to be altered or amended.

This was settled on the 18th of November, with one condition more, in regard to the custody of the person of the child during his infancy; as he dreaded that if Morabah had that custody it would in effect give him the power of government, and thereby the scene of troubles would be renewed, it was stipulated the care of his person should be committed to Perwetty Boy, and if she should refuse to accept, or after acceptance chuse to resign it, he should be disposed of in the manner most conducive to his safety, and the honour of the contracting parties. On the 27th of November he affixed his seal to this treaty. The council advanced him another lack of roupies, so that he received in the whole four lacks.

On receiving intelligence that the ministers at Poonah were making preparations to oppose the intended march, it was resolved to to expedite it; and Colonel Egerton aſſuring that every thing was ready, the troops were ordered to march out of the iſland the 22d of November. In the mean time all communication with the continent was ſtopped, and orders were ſent to Mr. Lewis to provide for his own ſafety.

Captain Stewart was with the firſt diviſion to proceed by the way of Apta and ſecure Bore Gaut, and Colonel Egerton himſelf was with the other diviſion, which had proceeded under the command of Colonel Cay, to ſeize Billapore.

On the 25th of November Captain Stewart had, without having met any oppoſition, taken poſſeſſion of the Gaut, and the fort of Candoli, where Mr. Lewis reached him in ſafety; and Colonel Egerton on the 26th encamped at Panwell with the remainder of the army.

By the inſtructions given to the committee on their proceeding to join the army, the line was drawn between their functions and thoſe of the commander, giving them the ſole management of all matters of negotia-

tion,

tion, the execution of the general plan of the expedition, and the determination of all points relative thereto; but they were prohibited from intermeddling in the detail of the duty of the army, the mode of march or encampment, or of carrying any military measure into execution.

On the 15th of December the whole army with the committee had reached Campoly, where intelligence was received that a body of ministerial forces, being 10,000 horse, with fifteen pieces of cannon, and a large number of Boudays, encamped at Worgaum, three coss on this side Tullingaum, to obstruct the march when the English should make their appearance above the Gauts, that 5000 horse were to proceed down the Cursora Gaut to cut off the communication with Panwell, and that Nanah, Saccaram, Sindia, and Furkia were encamped near Poonah with 5000 more. Their resolution was, by hovering about the army, without coming to a close engagement, to distress and wear them out. Ragobah was encamped near the English, and it was not doubted but a number of chiefs would soon appear with a force sufficient to remove all those threatened obstacles.

Though

Though it was now the 23d of December, the army had not proceeded further than Campoli. This immenſe delay was occaſioned by the making of roads for the cannon; Mr. Carnac remonſtrated againſt it, and propoſed that they ſhould be carried up by hand, which he argued was poſſible, as ſome artillery had already been paſſed that way. The commander treated this as chimerical, and they continued there, attacked now and then by ſome of the hovering troops, who, whenever they came near enough to be reached by the Engliſh army, were repulſed: it happened very unfortunately that in theſe ſkirmiſhes Colonel Cay was mortally wounded, and Captain Stewart killed. The loſs of thoſe two excellent officers was of great conſequence; at the ſame time Mr. Moſtyns illneſs, which had begun ſoon after he left Bombay, increaſed to ſuch a degree, that he was obliged to return thither, where he dyed the 1ſt of January: and Colonel Egerton found his ſtate of health ſo bad, that it diſabled him from attending either civil or military functions; in conſequence he reſigned the command of the army, in which Colonel Cockburn ſucceeded him. Major Dagon of the artillery was promoted to the rank of Lieutenant Colonel.

The Englifh force had now paffed the Gauts and reached Indorain. The reality of things proved far from anfwering the idea of fuccour they had flattered themfelves with at their fetting out. They had expected that as foon as they fhould have paffed the Gauts, Holcar and other chiefs of rank would have joined them with large bodies of horfe, by which, if they received no other fervice, provifions and forage from the country round would have been fecured: but no fuch appeared, nor any perfons but a few mercenaries. Ragobah faw he had been deceived, and owned, that unlefs they whom he reckoned on as friends were by the fpeedy defeat of his enemies affured of fafety, he could not reckon on their joining him. As the Englifh and he advanced towards Poonah, the difficulty of being fupplied from the Concan increafed, from the greater advantage given by the nature of the country to the flying parties, and the only hope left was that when they fhould approach very near to Poonah, Holcar might be enabled to fulfil his promifes. Other accidents concurred to increaſe the defection or coldneſs of Ragobah's partizans. Morabah confined in Ahmednagur, had been informed that Ragobah, inſtead of taking proper meaſures for his releaſe, had written to the Killedar of that fort, not to looſe him, until he ſhould ſend his orders from Poonah. This was ſoon ſpread, and whether true or falſe, had an effect fatal to his cauſe. Indeed it was plainly ſeen by the committee that Ragobahs aim was, by the Engliſh arms to force his way through all oppoſition, that ſo every body might be at his mercy.

The Bombay council, to facilitate ſupplies from the Concan, ſent a detachment of a company of Europeans, three of Sepoys, two field pieces and artillery men to clear the country between Panwell and Campoli; at the ſame time they exhorted the new commander Colonel Cockburn, to loſe no time, but proceed with vigour in his march.

Colonel Egerton, after his reſignation, had ſet out to return to Bombay; but the roads were ſo occupied by the roving parties of the Mahrattas, that finding it impoſſible to reach Panwell, he returned to the army, where he

 reſumed

resumed his place in the committee, but not in the command of the troops. The committee therefore now consisted of Mr. Carnac and him only. After a march of fifteen days, during which they were continually harrassed by numerous parties of horse, who, whenever they encamped came so near as to cannonade, but when attacked instantly retreated, the army reached Tullangaum, which was but eighteen miles from Poonah; the whole country was laid waste, and every thing that could not be carried off destroyed by fire. Tullangaum at their arrival was in flames; the same fate impended for Chinsura, and even Poonah. After a halt of two days at this place, where the enemy harrassed them in their wonted manner, the committee upon enquiry found there must speedily be a want of provisions, and the particular circumstances of their situation being considered by them, they determined that it was not possible for the army to proceed, but that they must retreat towards Bombay.

Upon this determination, Mr. Carnac sent for Colonel Cockburn, and informed him of it. The colonel remonstrated against it, alledging that the English troops used not to retreat but advance againſt the enemy, would be diſcouraged by ſuch a meaſure, which as it damped their ſpirit, muſt in proportion raiſe that of the Mahratta troops, who would not fail to attack them during the march; that if the Engliſh by ill fortune ſhould be at laſt forced to treat, they would inſiſt on very hard terms; whereas if a treaty was to be made, it were more advantageous to endeavour at it in the preſent ſituation when they were within eighteen miles of Poonah; that if permitted to continue the march, he had no doubt of carrying the army there. But the retreat was reſolved, and the order given. To have the advance of the enemy, the march was to begin at eleven o'clock that night; it was made in three diviſions; the troops, which as they marched forward were the advanced guard, now became the rear; they were commanded by Captain Hartley. The main body was incumbered by a great quantity of baggage, 1200 pack bullocks, 300 carts, a buzar, an artillery park, and 1000 coolies * with officer's baggage. The enemy ſurrounding on all ſides, amounted to more than 100,000, the Engliſh

* A ſpecies of the loweſt kind.

army originally not quite 4000, were somewhat diminished. Colonel Cockburn thought it proper to acquaint Ragobah with his design; by this the enemy were apprized of it, and about two in the morning the advanced guard was attacked; they had proceeded to a considerable distance from the main body, which had been retarded by dragging the baggage through very bad roads, this the enemy took a great part of. The attack was continued with vigour, but notwithstanding their reiterated charges, the advanced guard about daylight reached Worgaum, having saved most of their provision and ammunition. About four in the morning the main body was attacked on the rear and both flanks; the halt this occasioned gave the enemy the opportunity of bringing up cannon; the army then formed, and the attack became general about six. The weight of it fell on the rear guard, commanded by Captain Hartley; the conduct and courage of this gallant officer was answered by the bravery of his men. From the situation of this corps, and the distance of it from the main body, no support was given them till about twelve o'clock; during these six hours he sustained repeated charges, without being once broken. A

small

ſmall part of the European battalion was then ſent under Major Frederick, who had orders in every thing to act by the direction of Captain Hartley. The major choſe when he had joined the rear, to act in a private capacity, as a volunteer. Soon after this reinforcement had arrived, the order came for the whole to retire, and about four in the afternoon all the army had effected their retreat, and got to Worgaum, having loſt ſixty-three artillery, ſixty-two Engliſh, and two hundred and thirty-ſeven Sepoys.

During the halt at Tullangaum, Ragobah had for himſelf opened a negotiation with Sindia, and declared his intention of putting himſelf under his protection: he was received by him, and was at this time actually in his camp, where he was treated with reſpect.

The next day, the 15th, the committee had another conſultation on the diſmal ſituation of their affairs, and Colonel Cockburn being aſked his opinion, notwithſtanding the bravery ſhewn the preceding day, gave it under his hand that the troops would not ſtand ſuch another attack; that from the number

ber of the enemy and their reiterated attacks, they ſhould, through their many halts, be twenty days before they could reach Panwell, and muſt be totally deſtroyed; and he declared he could not charge himſelf with conducting the army to Bombay; in this opinion Colonel Egerton (though he did not ſet his hand to it) concurred. Upon this it was determined to try whether they could not, by treating with the Mahratta chiefs, extricate themſelves from the dreadful ſtreights to which they were reduced. As Nanah the miniſter, in whom the power oſtenſibly reſided, was then in the Mahratta camp, it was thought proper to ſend Mr. Farmer to him, to negotiate for an undiſturbed retreat of the army to Bombay. He at firſt was tolerably well received, and nothing more demanded than that the perſon of Ragobah ſhould be delivered up: but when that was found not poſſible even though the Engliſh chiefs ſhould yield to ſo humiliating a condition, Nanah's behaviour altered, he roſe in his demands, and inſiſted that the Engliſh ſhould ſurrender all the acquiſitions they had made ſince the time of Mahderow; that the detachment under Colonel Goddard ſhould be ordered to retreat to Bengal, and intimated that the Engliſh army muſt

muſt be detained where they then were, till the lands to be ceded by this treaty were delivered into the poſſeſſion of the Poonah Durbar. To this ſevere requiſition he added inſult; for Mr. Farmer was left in the open Buzar without any covering but his palanqueen, or any place in which he could write his meſſages. Theſe mortifying terms being come to the Engliſh camp, another conſultation was held; Mr. Carnac declared that at all hazards he ſhould prefer continuing their retreat rather than ſubmit to ſuch diſgraceful conditions; but as the military officers had given their opinions that it was impoſſible to effect it, he would not take upon himſelf to decide on his ſingly. In this emergency it occured to them, that Sindia having in ſome meaſure ſhewn himſelf favorable to the cauſe of Ragobah by his reception of him, might on this occaſion be ſerviceable to them. To try this, Mr. Holmes was ſent to him. On his way he was met by ſome of Nanah's troops, who, as they feared that this meſſage might prove to the advantage of the ſenders, and the diminution of their maſter's credit, endeavoured to prevent his acceſs to Sindia, firſt by requiring him to go to Nanah, and then detaining him till a party of Sindia's

Sindia's troops came and dispersed them, and carried him into their master's presence; there he was received with humanity and kindness. Sindia seemed flattered with this acknowledgment of his consequence; and upon Mr. Holmes, in his return of thanks for his civility, comparing his behaviour to Nanah's in regard to Mr. Farmer, he immediately sent for him, and desired that both he and Mr. Holmes would look on themselves as his guests. They then begun to treat with him on the subject of their mission, in the first place shewing a writing signed by the committee, wherein they declared they had not power to grant such terms as the Durbar in the person of Nanah had prescribed: that such a treaty would be a nullity, and that should they be compelled to sign such a convention, the ministers would be deceived if they trusted to it. This declaration was also presented to Nanah, who would hear of no diminution of what he had required; he even sent a message to Sindia desiring that he would not recede from that point of retaining the army, but moreover require particularly the surrender of the castle of Surat and Fort Victoria, and the payment of the expences of the war, before they should be released; and at at the ſame time he ſent orders to Furkia to take the proper meaſures for preventing their eſcape. Mr. Holmes promiſed Sindia, that if he would befriend the Engliſh in this matter, the council of Bombay would cede to him Broach and its Pergunnah which had been conquered by them from the Nabob of Surat. Sindia did effectually endeavour to leſſen the hardſhip of the terms impoſed, but prevailed only in regard to the releaſe of the army. He prevented the orders given to Furkia from being executed, but leſt he ſhould diſpleaſe the other Mahratta chiefs required that hoſtages ſhould be given for the performance of the ſtipulated ceſſion.

Hard as theſe conditions were, they ſeemed to the committee preferable to the loſs of the army, which they looked on as inevitable ſhould the Mahratta chiefs be thoroughly acquainted with the deſpondency of the leaders; they feared that Sindia, apprehenſive of loſing his influence with thoſe chiefs, who, ſenſible of the advantage this occaſion had given him muſt wonder at his neglect of it, might through that and the reiterated inſtances of Nanah, be prevailed on to come into and ſecond his rigorous conditions, perhaps,

if

if angered by resistance enhance them; and relying on the effect of the express declaration so solemnly given under their hands, that they had not power to accede to such terms, and that whatever they thus were compelled to do, would be a nullity, they consented to sign a convention, whereby all that had been acquired by the Bombay council since the time of Mahderow was to be surrendered, and orders to be sent to Colonel Goddard to conduct his detachment back to Bengal: and Mr. Farmer and Lieutenant Stewart were to remain as hostages for the performance of these conditions. This done the army was permitted to retreat to Bombay, escorted by a detachment of horse: Ragobah remained under the protection of Sindia. Mr. Holmes thought it proper to be munificent in presents to Sindia's officers, but not having ready cash made his present in bills and notes payable at Bombay, amounting to 41,000 roupies.

The feelings of men now reduced to be guarded by those very troops they had been accustomed to behold flying before them, can be more easily imagined than described: by the time they reached Bombay, the joy caused by their safety had given way to indignation

at

at the ſhame and diſgrace brought on the British arms.

On the 29th of January the council met at Bombay, in which Colonel Egerton and Colonel Cockburn reſumed their ſeats. The firſt thing done was reading the diary of the unfortunate expedition; after which Mr. Hornby repreſented that the cauſes of the failure of it might be matter of future conſideration, that they ſhould now proceed to determine what meaſures were to be taken for their ſafety, and retrieving their affairs. He arraigned the conduct of the leaders whilſt he extolled the bravery of the army, and inſiſted that to keep up that gallant ſpirit they had ſhewn, it was neceſſary to diſtinguiſh thoſe who had done them honour from thoſe who had been wanting in their duty, whoſe example was pernicious: he mentioned ſome inferior officers to be tried by courts martial, at the ſame time he impeached the conduct of Colonel Egerton and Colonel Cockburn, and offered it as his opinion, that until their behaviour could be fully enquired into, they ſhould decline acting in a military character; his charge was particularly in regard to the opinion Colonel Cockburn ſigned at Worgaum,

gaum, in which Colonel Egerton had concurred. If they did not conſent to what he propoſed, he ſhould move for their ſuſpenſion. Colonel Egerton at firſt inſiſted on keeping his place both in the army and the council till a formal charge was delivered againſt him, but upon further conſideration he, as well as Colonel Cockburn, acquieſced, and they declined acting in their military capacity until the opinion of the ſupreme council ſhould be known.

It is not ſurprizing that after ſo diſagreeable an event the actors ſhould endeavour each to throw the blame from himſelf. The compaſs of this work will not permit deſcending to many particulars of this altercation, which appears at length in the minutes of the Bombay council.

Mr. Carnac blamed the ſlowneſs with which the army proceeded from Panwell, and to that attributed the greatneſs of that force to which they were obliged to yield; and as to the retreat, he affirmed that there was no poſſibility of acting otherwiſe as things were then circumſtanced; he blamed the diſtance of the diviſions whereby they were unable to

ſupport

ſupport each other, and the not having ordered the ſecond diviſion to ſupport the rear when attacked, which he affirmed might have been eaſily done; and as to the determination at Worgaum, he ſaid that his own private opinion was againſt it; but that although, by his caſting vote in the committee, he might have prevented it, he did not think his authority extended ſo far as to give orders for the march at all events; and though it had, it would have been imprudent to give it to officers who had expreſſed ſuch an opinion of the troops they were to lead. That there was no alternative, no way left, but to obtain the beſt terms poſſible for the unmoleſted return of the army to Bombay.

Colonel Egerton juſtified the delay attributed to him by Mr. Carnac, from the impoſſibility of dragging the artillery through roads impaſſable till mended by the labourers; from the time neceſſarily conſumed in getting proviſions: and he poſitively denied that he had refuſed conducting the army from Worgaum to Bombay, or having concurred in Colonel Cockburn's written opinion, which he did not remember ſo much as to have ſeen till it was produced at that board.

Colonel

Colonel Cockburn laid all the miſcarriage on the firſt error in ordering the retreat. He ſet forth in his juſtification the remonſtrance he had made againſt it; his undertaking, if the army marched forward, to conduct it to Poonah; that the diſtance of the diviſions was occaſioned by the quantity of baggage, and the badneſs of the ground through which they were to march, whereby the firſt diviſion, unencumbered, was enabled to advance more quickly than the others; that as ſoon as poſſible he had ſent relief to Captain Hartley. He owned the opinion he had ſigned, and ſaid, that it was founded on the information he had received from ſepoy officers that their men and black officers were likely to deſert in the night, which was confirmed by meſſages received from Ragobah and Mr. Sibbald; that ſome deſertion did actually happen; that ſuch another attack would have exhauſted the ammunition; that the great difficulty of carrying three hundred ſick men would have increaſed their embarraſſments; that the army, already diminiſhed in numbers, having ſo many attacks to ſuſtain, muſt have totally periſhed ere they could have reached Panwell: theſe were the grounds of his opinion, notwithſtanding which he would, to to the best of his ability, had Mr. Carnac, by his casting vote ordered the retreat to be continued, have led the army; that by saying he could not charge himself with the conduct of the army, he did not mean to refuse conducting it, if such an order had been given, but merely to avoid responsibility for the ill success which he foresaw; that Colonel Dagon was of the same opinion; why was he therefore accused as the cause of a measure which depended on others?

Captain Hartley was, for his service on the retreat, promoted to the rank of Lieutenant Colonel; this occasioned complaints and remonstrances from the other officers; but those things are not of a nature to be dwelt on here *.

* In the letter to the secret committee, the council of Bombay enter very fully into the reasons for the advancement of Colonel Hartley, and mention not only his conduct on the retreat, which saved the whole army, but his spirited advice when consulted at Worgaum, where he insisted, when desertion was mentioned, that he could depend on the men he commanded, that he had effectually prevented desertion from spreading in his corps; he urged every argument for continuing the retreat rather than submit to disgraceful terms. He even formed a disposition, and presented it to Colonel Cockburn for conducting it, and avoiding the inconveniencies of a night march, and the division of the troops. He hath since shewn himself worthy of his advancement.

The return of the army to Bombay was immediately followed by the arrival of a Vaqueel from the Poonah Durbar, and one separately on the part of Sindia, demanding in form the poſſeſſion of the ſeveral places ſtipulated to be ſurrendered; the anſwer given was, that Meſſ. Carnac and Egerton had no authority to conclude any treaty on behalf of the Company, that this had been declared to the leaders of the Mahrattas before the paper upon which they grounded their demand was ſubſcribed, and that the Bombay council had no authority to take any ſteps in conſequence until they received the ſentiments of the Supreme Council, to whom they would diſpatch a veſſel, and wait their determination. Care was taken at the ſame time to leave an opening for treating ſeparately with Sindia.

On the 19th of February the Bombay council took into conſideration the ſtate of their affairs. The preſident Mr. Hornby laid before them a minute on that ſubject, in which he entered into a full detail of all facts and circumſtances. He mentioned, in the firſt place, the attention they ſhould have paid to Colonel Goddard's army, and informed them that it had reached Brampour the

the 29th of January: he added, that there was no danger of a Mahratta army marching against him, as they were too busy at home: that they were already sending troops to the neighbourhood of Carange and Salcet, being resolved to obtain the cession of all promised by the convention of Wargaum, which they had demanded the possession of by their Vaqueels. He represented that as it was to be expected, that Nanah would lose no time in proceeding to enforce the cession he demanded, they ought to lose no time in their preparations to resist him. He then entered into a detail of what had passed previous to that convention, lamenting the bad effects of discontinuing a march which would have been equal to a victory: he mentioned all the particulars relating to Sindia's behaviour when applied to by Mr. Holmes, as a proof of his inclination to be on good terms with the English, not only on account of the promise made to him of Broach and the share of its Pergunnah, but from political future views, which he deduced from the several incidents at the time of the convention and soon after, and from the circumstances in which all matters stood at that moment. He mentioned that Mr. Holmes during his residence in Sindia's camp, had obſerved that all affairs of importance were determined by him though they were oſtenſibly referred to Nanah, who in virtue of his office was to affix the ſeal to the orders, but this was never done till Sindia had examined and paſſed them: that Holcar, though treated outwardly with the reſpect and form due to the firſt Subahdar of the empire, was totally at his diſpoſal: that Sindia had acquieſced in ſending hoſtages to Bombay in exchange for the Engliſh who remained with him, and had taken that occaſion of ſending a confidential perſon to the preſident: that Mr. Holmes, who was returned to Bombay was charged with the moſt friendly aſſurances from him: that Mr. Farmer, who remained with him, was treated with kindneſs; that he permitted no intercourſe between him and Nanah; that he had the command of Nanah's and Holcar's force as well as his own. He then informed the council of what had paſſed between the Mahratta chiefs after the retreat of the Engliſh, and the diſpoſition of the ſeveral departments of their government; which were,

1. The infant Madherow Narrain was to be acknowledged Paiſhwa.

2. Sevagi

2. Sevagi Badgerow (a ſon of Ragobah, born to him ſince the adoption of Amrut Row, and) an infant of very tender years, to be Naib, and that the exerciſe of his office ſhould be carried on in his name by Sindia and Holcar.

3. That Ragobah ſhould totally relinquiſh all claim to government, and have a jaghire and reſide at Jaſſi; that he ſhould ſignify in writing to all the powers in India, that he accepted and agreed to this condition.

4. That Nanah and Saccaram ſhould act as miniſters, but derive their authority totally from Sindia and Holcar. Theſe ſeveral articles were, he ſaid, ſolemnly agreed to by all the chiefs.

He then mentioned inſtances of Sindia's diſpoſition to a ſeparate alliance with the Engliſh; that he was more inclined to grant Mr. Moſtyn's requiſitions than even Morabah; that his averſion to a French alliance was known, having formerly made advances repeatedly, and in Mr. Moſtyn's abſence, ſent Appagee Sapagou, the very perſon then in Bombay, to Mr. Lewis, who knowing that meaſures were already taken with Ragobah could go no further, than to make general profeſſions of friendſhip; that Appagee avoided all meeting with the agent ſent by Nanah, and had in charge only the particular intereſts of Sindia: that he never mentioned the return of the Bengal detachment; and what was very remarkable, though the order from Meſſ. Carnac and Egerton to Colonel Goddard for that purpoſe had been delivered to him to be ſent, they had no account of its having been yet received *.

From theſe ſeveral facts he reaſoned on the motives which cauſed them; that the the principal view of Sindia muſt be to retain his power at Poonah; that he had to dread the jealouſy of the other chiefs, neceſſarily fearing his power, and the uſe he, when fully eſtabliſhed, might make of it in cruſhing them; that the Nizam and Hyder

* Meſſ. Carnac and Egerton wrote from Campoli the 19th of January 1779, that he was to pay no regard to their order of the 16th, becauſe, upon recollection, they found they were not authorized to give it. This he received at Burhampore the 2d of February, and the order of the 16th of January he only received the 9th of February in his camp at Chopwah upon the Gutnuddy, by a Vaqueel belonging to the infant Paiſhwa.

were

were ready to ſupport them againſt him. The influence of the Bramins, through the aſcendancy of their caſt, and their great wealth, was another ſource of uneaſineſs to him: that however great his power whilſt he was at or near Poonah with his troops, his abſence from thence would afford opportunities to thoſe who felt the weight of it to ſhake it off, which dangers made his preſence neceſſary; whilſt on the other hand his private concerns ſuffered by his abſence from his own dominions: that the King had taken occaſion from it to ſeize ſome forts belonging to him; that he feared both the Nizam's and Hyder's attempts of the ſame kind; that he had ſome uneaſineſs alſo in regard to Modagee Bouncelo, whoſe intereſts croſſing his, muſt be apprehenſive of his power; that if Nanah, at liberty by this abſence to exerciſe his talents and influence, ſhould regain the ſuperiority, he would, by the French alliance be enabled to keep it. From the detail of all theſe conſiderations he drew the following concluſions:

1. That the actual adminiſtration of affairs in the Mahratta empire was at Sindia's

 diſpoſal;

disposal; that Nanah was reduced to be no more than the tool of his power.

2. That Sindia was not only inclined to the English in preference to the French, but earnest for some closer connexion, and alliance with the English.

3. That the accomplishment of the terms of the convention, so far as related to the Poonah sircar, was not the object of his views, since he had in fact given the English the option whether to comply with them or not.

4. That the performance even of the private article in his favour was not the first object of his consideration; but chiefly intended as a fund to pay from in any alliance.

5. That independently of his views to an alliance he had some motives of policy, which rendered him unwilling that the English possessions and power on that coast should be materially reduced.

6. That it was for the interest of the Company, and necessary to their purposes at this settlement, to find what Sindia's

real

real intentions were, and to take meaſures in concert with him for the excluſion of Nanah from all power.

His reaſons for his ſuppoſitions were, that all dominion but that of the ſword was overthrown at Poonah; that Sindia being then in poſſeſſion of it, his great object muſt have been to ſecure it, and his intention either to remove the ſeat of his government to Poonah, or to eſtabliſh there ſome power ſubordinate to his. That the firſt was dangerous, and would alarm all the chiefs who aimed to continue their independence, as his great power muſt enable him to cruſh them. The Nizam and Hyder would be ever ready to ſupport them in the ſouthern parts of the empire, where the Bramins have great weight from the circumſtances of caſt, riches, and influence. In Sindia's own jaghire, the king taking advantage of his and Holcar's abſence, was making ſome progreſs againſt them; that Modagee looked to the Rajaſhip; that the king and he muſt be conſidered as dangerous enemies to Sindia. As to the ſecond, the eſtabliſhment of a ſubordinate power that ſeemed more ſuitable to his circumſtances and agreeable to his paſt conduct.

duct. The difficulty lay in the means: his choice of Nanah to be Duan aroſe from his hope of gaining credit by the moderation ſhewn in placing in that office a man of ſuch abilities, and of the Bramin caſt; but this choice was dangerous by the occaſion his abſence and Holcar's alſo (whoſe affairs called him away) furniſhed Nanah to aſſert his independence, and continue his connexions with St. Lubin; that the arrival of the aſſiſtance from France would reſtore his ſuperiority, but the ſupport of the Engliſh power on the coaſt was a ſecurity againſt even his independence; that the Bramins in general were inclined to the French; that even Morabah was ſo; that it was the mutual intereſt of both Sindia and the Engliſh to guard againſt Nanah and their influence; that the council was bound in honour to acquit themſelves to him, his protection at Worgaum being a valuable conſideration; that Ragobah by his engagement with Sindia had relieved the Company from the care of his intereſts; and that all ſtipulations tending to be hoſtile to Berar were to be avoided. He therefore, in the firſt place, propoſed that the notes given by Mr. Holmes among Sindia's officers as Durbar charges, amounting

ing to 41,000 roupies, ſhould be immediately paid.

In the mean time every thing was to be prepared ſo as to be in readineſs for ſervice, that if Sindia ſhould refuſe their advances an army might be ſent into the field toward Surat or Broach, to act in concert with the detachment; that an alliance with the Guicawars ſhould be attempted; that ſuch a connection was deſirable from their command of the Guzerat, their averſion to the Poonah government, and their diſtance from the center of the empire; that the diviſions which then reigned among them diminiſhed their importance; that the connexion Futty Sing had with Sindia ſhould incline them to him; that an alliance with Sindia was in every reſpect preferable to one with Modagee Bouncello, as the claims he had upon the ſucceſſion to the Rajaſhip tended to create embarraſſments.

"That as to Ragobah there could be no thought of purſuing the plan of his reſtoration: that circumſtances differed totally from what they were in the year 1775, when ſervice was tendered to him by Sindia, who now had the

the command of an army, the only title to the empire, that Ragobah was his pensioner, and merely a cloak to his ambition. Upon this representation it was resolved,

That the convention at Worgaum was invalid; and that as after the express declaration to the Durbar, that the committee had not the power to accede to those terms, the public faith could not be considered as pledged; that the general answer already given to Nanah was all then necessary.

That Sindia, in consequence of his good offices, was entitled to every mark of regard, and that it was necessary to find some equivalent to the cession of the Mogul share of the Broach Pergunnah;

That the notes given for 41,000 roupies Durbar charges should be forthwith paid;

That there was good ground to hope Sindia is well disposed to and willing to enter into a connexion with the Company;

That the object in this connexion must be,

1. The

1. The total exclusion of the French, and of Nanah from any share in the government at Poonah.

2. To preserve for the Company the territory they then held.

That it was absolutely necessary to lose no time in endeavouring at this, and to avoid any engagement hostile to the Raja of Berar; that nothing should be finally settled without the concurrence of the Governor and Supreme Council; that in consequence of these resolutions the president should write to Sindia.

Although the reflexions of Mr. Hornby were in general well founded, he was mistaken in two points: the Durbar at Poonah were not inattentive to Colonel Goddard's march; they had actually detached 20,000 of their best horse to surprize him, but his celerity in his progress from Brampour prevented their reaching him, they therefore returned without having committed any act of hostility. Nor was Sindia so well inclined to the English or naturally averse to a French alliance: though he had granted passes for the march of the detachment through his country,

country, and made no hostile opposition, he had thrown obstacles in their way, by ordering the merchants to remove from Brampour, whereby it became difficult for Colonel Goddard to raise money on his bills. This manner of acting was consistent with the policy that guides the princes of Indostan; whatever dissentions reign among them, they all unite in hatred of Europeans, and most of the English whom they fear: this is their natural bent. Their seeming present interest, or the views of their minister, either for their masters or their own private advantage, often predominates over that bias; by those channels only they are accessible. The president in consequence of the resolutions wrote to Sindia, but he did not meet those advances in the manner hoped for. The demands of the stipulated cessions were reiterated, the delay occasioned by writing to the Supreme Council was complained of as an evasion; effects followed these messages, a body of their troops advanced to fort Victoria, and intelligence was received of preparations for the attack of Salcet. Proper precautions taken prevented their effecting their purposes.

The

The happy arrival of Colonel Goddard with his detachment at Surat, on the 25th of February, changed the face of affairs. It is now time to revert to the proceedings of the Supreme Council and the march of that detachment; but before we enter upon that ſubject, it may not be amiſs to enquire into the cauſe of the remarkable event juſt related: a gallant army, after a defence as glorious as a victory, reduced humbly to crave and ſubmit to diſgraceful terms, and retire, covered with ſhame, to the place whence they had ſet out, pluming themſelves in full aſſurance of returning crowned with ſucceſs, and the honour of giving a ruler to the Mahratta empire. The character of the prince whom they eſpouſed, and the views of thoſe who eſpouſed him, lead to it. The true way of judging mens characters is not to decide upon the events of their lives, but upon their behaviour in conſequence of theſe events. Thoſe in the life of Ragobah are various, and ſome of them ſurprizing; from the begining to end he hath been the ſport of Fortune in all her inconſtancy. The changes from ill to good ſeem to be the effect of the policy of the Mahratta chiefs, and thoſe from proſperity to wretchedneſs, the effect of oſcitancy,

tancy, and ſudden impreſſions of fear precipitate in their exertion. Naturally bold and brave he formed ſchemes of greatneſs, and entered upon them with ſpirit; but looking to one object only, he ſaw not the obſtacles that lay in his way, or the thorns that might render his paſſage difficult, yet he was prone to ſuſpicion, which, when once admitted, totally abſorbed every idea but that of the danger it pointed out, and hurried him to decide merely on that idea, without examining whether it was well founded or groundleſs. At the ſame time as prone to truſt thoſe to whom he applied in ſuch emergencies without knowing whether they were well or ill inclined to him: he had talents of generalſhip which he exerted with ſucceſs; his errors in forming his deſigns ſeem to have ariſen from an over-weening impatience which prevented his examination of the probability that the promiſes of his friends, and the warmth of his expectation, would be anſwered; this made him venture raſhly, and urge with impetuoſity thoſe on whom he could really depend, not conſidering that if by yielding to that raſhneſs their ſtrength was broken, he loſt his only ſupport; that impetuoſity made him ſuppoſe his wiſh completed when the firſt

first step towards it was scarcely taken, and forget that he owed attentions to those who had already favoured or might in future favour his cause, and act as if he was really seated in the fullness of power and no more wanted their assistance, or feared their enmity; he saw not the true reason of his so readily meeting support in his ill fortune, that the princes who then espoused his cause did it not from any persuasion of the justice of it, or any affection to his person, but merely from policy, their independence being preserved by the continuation of the dissentions which the Mahratta empire; during which they could not be called to account for their tribute, as the side they befriended would not, and that they opposed, could not enforce payment of it: this system accounts for the general run of the acts of the Mahratta chiefs. This it was which raised him armies in his former distresses, and influenced Sindia to receive him when the English army retreated from Tullinghaum, and to soften the rigour of Nanah's requisition at Worgaum; he had no reason to fear their prosperity, and knew, by experience, that a complete settlement of the empire, under the Duanship of Nana, and ministry of the Bramins,

mins, would extinguiſh his influence, and that as ſoon as they found themſelves eſtabliſhed in their poſts, and ſtrengthened in credit by an increaſe of territory, they would demand and enforce the payment of the arrears of tribute: this muſt have been the firſt thought that ſtruck him on the application of Mr. Holmes, the ſending his vaqueel to Bombay, with particular inſtructions on his ſeparate intereſt, plainly proves it: he meant to have Ragobah under his protection, or rather in his cuſtody, that he might upon occaſion make a proper uſe of that circumſtance.

Unfortunately the impatience of Ragobah was communicated to the greateſt part of the Bombay council; like him, too eaſily truſting to outward appearance, they imagined themſelves at Poonah from the moment the miniſtry quarrelled; the many tergiverſations and uncertainties which reigned in that Durbar did not open their eyes. Upon the firſt proſpect of ſucceſs attending Ragobah's party, or rather thoſe who uſed his name to compaſs their ends in depriving their enemies of the power they aimed to aſſume, they abandoned themſelves to the flattering ſcene of importance

importance and credit accruing to them from ſettling and giving a chief to an empire, and feared nothing but the diminution of glory which they might ſuffer from other perſons having a ſhare in the enterprize. This muſt have been the motive of their forbidding the advance of the Bengal detachment by their firſt orders, as well that of their hurry in planning and in executing the accompaniment of Ragobah and reinſtating him in the regency, although they knew that by the confinement of Morabah, Butchaba and their adherents, and the ſmall degree of power Holcar had, the principal force on which they had reckoned would be wanting.

Their impatience exceeded that of Ragobah; to prevent delay by his objections to the treaty, they increaſed the ſums advanced to him; the march of the detachment and its daily progreſs was known to them, they might have calculated the diſtance which each day diminiſhed, and by a ſettled correſpondence with Colonel Goddard, have carried on their plan ſo that he might have co-operated with them; with this precaution ſucceſs was certain, but then the honour of that ſucceſs muſt have been attributed to his ſkill in the execution, and the wiſdom of the Supreme council in ſending that detachment to their aſſiſtance: this was a meaſure from the beginning diſagreeable to them, they were angered by the firſt interpoſition of that council which produced the treaty of Poounder, and that reſentment was kept up by the exerciſe of the ſuperiority given by the act of parliament; this appears through their minutes of council, and thoſe ſentiments helped to ſtrengthen the others *.

The ill-timed order given by Ragobah for the continuation of Morabah's confinement was another fatal ſtep; the act itſelf might be called ingratitude to the man who firſt ſtirred in his favour, when he ſeemed forgotten and excluded for ever from all chance

* In juſtice to Mr. Draper, one of the members of the Bombay council, it muſt not be omitted that he diſſented not only from the firſt reſolution to forbid the advance of the detachment, but alſo from that of the 12th of October 1778, for conducting Ragobah to Poonah with an armed force; he grounded this diſſention on, 1ſt. Their departure from the conditions preſcribed by the ſupreme council, "That their plan ſhould not interfere with any engagement formed with Modagee; that by advice from Europe, they ſhould be aſſured that the force they ſent could be ſpared without danger, that their engagements with Ragobah or Morabah ſhould not be hoſtile to the "Rajah

chance of a return to power; and it ſhewed a diſpoſition of mind which made not only Morabah's friends averſe to him, but ſtruck the other Indian chiefs as an indication of his deſign to govern with the ſame ſtrictneſs he had before done, when his title in the minority of his nephews to the regency, and after the death of Naron to the Paiſhwaſhip was undiſputed: this would have totally put an end to their ſcheme of independence, the maintenance of which is the moſt deſirable thing for the inhabitants of the diſtricts reſpectively bordering on the Mahratta dominions, and the particular intereſt of the Engliſh government in that region. The ſituation of the countries of theſe princes ſhews the probability of ſucceſs in a ſyſtem

"Rajah of Berar."—2d. Morabah and Butchaba being ſtill under reſtraint.—3d. The diſtance of the detachment being yet too great.—4th. There being a great deficiency in the European force from the eſtabliſhment ordered by the company,—he added, that although he was convinced of the neceſſity of removing Nanah, and reinſtating Ragobah in the regency, it appeared to him that it might be effected with more propriety and greater probability of ſucceſs, in about two months, as by that time they might hope the reſtrictions, with reſpect to the Berar negociation, might be removed, and the detachment might arrive at the deſtination ordered in July (in the neighbourhood of Poonah) and the company's ſhips and the ſquadron might be with them.

 formed

formed for that purpoſe. Separate treaties with each would ſtrengthen and enable them to reſiſt the force of the Poonah Durbar, which they would not fail to do when they found themſelves ſupported by Engliſh arms.

The proceedings of the council of Bombay have been related without the interference of other matters, that by an uninterrupted narration they might appear clearly: it will be neceſſary to reſume thoſe of the Supreme Council, and the acts in conſequence, particularly the march of the detachment commanded by Colonel Leſlie through the heart of Indoſtan; a meaſure of high importance, the effect of ſchemes long revolved in the mind of its author, bold in its conception, and continued with perſeverance from the conviction of its utility: the events finally produced by it muſt decide whether raſh and precipitate, or political and truly calculated for the good of the company, as well as for the fame attendant on ſo high an enterprize.

This meaſure had not paſſed in council without great debate. From its novelty, the

(the uſual manner of ſending troops having been by ſea) the general ignorance of the country to be paſſed over, and of the relations and intereſts of its princes and chiefs, the apparent danger from the heat of the climate, the delay which muſt be occaſioned by the rains, the inconvenience and difficulties which might ariſe from want of proviſions and aſſiſtance from the powers of the country or perhaps from their oppoſition, it was looked on as impracticable; but for the reaſons above related the council determined it not only practicable but expedient. The neceſſary precautions were taken with the princes of the countries through which the detachment was to paſs by apprizing them of the deſign of its march, and its pacific diſpoſitions to them, and requeſting their aſſiſtance in furniſhing proviſions: particularly letters were written to the Paiſhwa and his miniſtry fully mentioning theſe matters, and Mr. Moſtyn was inſtructed to aſſure them of the council's reſolution to abide by the treaty of Porounder, to explain the neceſſity of protecting the ſettlement of Bombay from foreign invaſion, and to deſire they would give orders to their chiefs dependent on the Paiſhwa not to moleſt the army in their march, but to ſupply

 them

them with what aſſiſtance they might ſtand in need of.

On the 23d of February 1778, reſolutions having paſſed in council for the appointment of Colonel Leſlie to this command, orders were iſſued in conſequence for the troops to aſſemble on the weſtern frontier of the province of Owde, either at Corah or in the neighbourhood of Culpee, as the commanding officer might chuſe.

Each ſepoy battalion conſiſted of ſeven hundred men, rank and file, one captain, ten ſubalterns Europeans, with the uſual number of native officers; and two pieces of artillery, ſix pounders, were attached to each battalion.

The regiment of cavalry conſiſted of five hundred natives, commanded by Captain Wray; the body of horſe from the province of Owde was compoſed of natives of the province of Candahar, and was of the ſame ſtrength: this corps had been in the ſervice of the late Sujah Dowlah Nabob of that province, and was continued by his ſon. It was commanded by a very gallant officer, who was alſo a native of Candahar.

The

The artillery consisted of four light twelve pounders, and two howitzers, besides the two six pounders above-mentioned attached to each battalion of sepoys: it was commanded by Major Baillie, one captain, and four subalterns, and a company of natives were appointed for the service of the whole.

Lieutenant Colonel Fortman was field engineer, with an assistant, a quarter-master-general and deputy; and all the other officers belonging to the staff, and persons necessary to be employed in the several departments of stores and provisions were named and chosen by the commander; to whom likewise unlimited authority was given to order such stores, and in such quantities, as he might deem necessary for that service.

On the 12th of April, the first division of the troops arrived at their rendezvous at Corah, where the whole were assembled on the 25th, when Colonel Leslie joined. From the 5th of May to the 18th, the troops were filing off by detachments, with their baggage and stores, to a pass on the banks of the Jumna, opposite Culpee. The distance between Corah and Culpee is about forty miles; that river

river forms the weſtern boundary of the dominions of the Nabob of Owde.

The town and fort of Culpee, which ſtand on the other ſide of the river, are the eaſtern boundary, of a ſmall diſtrict, bordering on the Bettwah Nullah*, on the other ſide of which lies the Boondelchund country, beginning at Jallapoor. This diſtrict was poſſeſſed by Gungadur Punt, the commander of the Mahratta force in that part of Indoſtan: he had received orders from Nanah to uſe all his endeavours to prevent the progreſs of the Engliſh march. He had with him his brother Ballagee, whoſe dominions were further to the weſt, and through which the route of the detachment lay. This man had great power and influence over his brother, and through the whole country, his cunning was great, and he laid the ſcheme of obſtructing us by every way preferably to arms, and to have recourſe to thoſe when his deception failed of ſucceſs: in conſequence vaqueels were ſent from both theſe chiefs to Colonel Leſlie with aſſurances of their maſters conſent and concurrence

* Nullah is a cut from a river by which grounds are watered.

currence to the march of the detachment, with the promiſe of a plentiful ſupply of proviſions through their country, and Ballagee adviſed him to go to the Nebuddah by the way of Mow, and offered himſelf to be his conductor. Colonel Leſlie not yielding to theſe ſpecious appearances, determined to proceed warily, for their vaqueels were not impowered to conclude any treaty, or even to treat, therefore every thing was vague and ſuſpicious. The governor of the fort of Culpee by his behaviour ſhewed how neceſſary caution was, and how little declarations were to be relied on. Application had been made to him for the aid of his boats in paſſing the river; this he not only refuſed, but as the workmen were employed in repairing thoſe which had been collected, a party detached from the fort began to fire on them; this was returned by the covering party, which with a few rounds from two pieces of artillery, obliged them to retire.

Colonel Leſlie ſending for the vaqueels, who were ſtill in camp, repreſented to them the treachery of ſuch conduct, and at the ſame time informed them of his intentions to croſs the river next day; the vaqueels made

made excuſes, begged for another day's delay, and propoſed that he ſhould croſs two and thirty miles higher up the river; Colonel Leſlie rejected this propoſal, adding his reaſons, with which they ſeemed perfectly ſatisfied, and deſired leave to go and inform their maſters, promiſing to return in the evening with an anſwer, which not being performed, gave cauſe to ſuſpect that ſome oppoſition would be made to the paſſage of the river.

The next morning, the 19th of May, at dawn of day, three battalions of ſepoys the firſt, fourth, and ſeventh, with their artillery arrived at the paſs. The firſt diviſion croſſed the river, and immediately formed; Colonel Goddard who commanded, ſeeing ſome troops aſſembling in his front, ſent a meſſage to their chief, deſiring to paſs unmoleſted; the anſwer was, that they ſhould come on: yet ſome ſmall bodies of cavalry began to fire at a diſtance on thoſe troops that were croſſing and forming. This was endured, until ſome were wounded; batteries which had been placed to cover the landing of the troops were then opened, which very ſoon diſperſed the enemy. That part of the troops

troops which had now paſſed were ordered to advance towards the village of Culpee, which was about a mile diſtant, and Major Fullerton, with the grenadiers, to prevent any ſurprize, was directed to make a movement to the left, but rather on their rear, both parties directing their march towards the village, where they were to unite. From the place whence the grenadiers had made their movement, the ground they had to paſs through was broken and uneven, with high banks and ravins, and the road ſo intricate, that, after marching ſome time, they found themſelves at a greater diſtance from the village than when they firſt moved; they were then very briſkly attacked by a body of about twelve hundred Mahratta horſe. The men behaved with great ſpirit and coolneſs, in particular the grenadiers of the fourth battalion. They began however to be preſſed when the other part of that battalion with its artillery, ſupported by the ſeventh, came from the village to their aſſiſtance, and ſoon decided the conteſt. The enemy retreated with the greateſt precipitation to a fort about ſix miles diſtant, where they had ſent their effects, and the troops were too much fatigued to purſue. A few grenadier ſepoys were wounded;

wounded; the loss of the enemy was much more considerable, and quiet possession was taken of the fort and village of Culpee, which they had evacuated.

This first act of hostility was followed by another vaqueel from the two chiefs, disavowing all knowledge of what had passed, promising to punish the offenders, and soliciting friendship. Colonel Leslie desirous of adhering to the spirit of his instructions, accepted their excuses, proposed terms of agreement, and while these were adjusting, the remainder of the detachment, with the artillery, baggage, and stores, crossed the river. The terms of the agreement were, that the troops should have an unmolested passage, that they should be supplied with provisions and necessaries at a proper price, and that the fort of Culpee should be kept by an English guard, as a security for the performance of of the agreement. The possession of it to be returned when the detachment had reached Chatterpore.

At this juncture a letter was received from the president and council of Bombay, with directions for the detachment to halt until further

further orders, without mentioning any reason for so unexpected a measure: advices of this, with an account of the agreement, followed those of the skirmish which had been communicated by Colonel Leslie to the Supreme Council. He informed them at the same time, that as the ground about Culpee would not admit of an encampment, without great inconvenience, he would move about twenty miles further to the banks of the Betwah Nullah, a good situation, on the frontiers of the Boondelchund country, where he would wait their further directions.

The Supreme Council had in the begining of May received letters from Bombay and Poonah, relating the revolutions in that Durbar, when Morabah and the other chiefs had in all likelihood overturned Nanah and Saccaram, and become the masters of that government, and afterwards had come to an agreement with them as before related. The Bombay council in their letters lamented that they should have so little share in the restoration of Ragobah, and that it should appear it could be effected without their assistance. These letters gave occasion to debates: a conclusion was drawn from them, that the reestablishment

eſtabliſhment of Ragobah was actually effected, which event muſt totally defeat any ſchemes the French might have formed, and put an end to the negotiations of Nanah with them, whereby the further progreſs of the detachment became unneceſſary. It was therefore propoſed, that orders ſhould be ſent to Colonel Leſlie to ſuſpend his march, or if he had proceeded in it, to return to Culpee. But upon conſideration that it d.d not from thoſe letters appear that the affairs of the company in that part of India were in ſuch ſecurity as not to require aid, but on the contrary that the connexions of the French with the Mahratta Durbar were yet ſubſiſting, St. Lubin ſtill reſiding at Poonah, and the veſſel which brought him into that country, and had been freighted for China accompanying General Belcombe inſtead of purſuing that voyage, being a ſtrong proof that he had entered into the deſign, and probably had gone himſelf to conduct or forward the negotiation; nor did the ıevolution appear certain, and if it was completed without the aid of the Bombay council, the ſettlement could not be permanent; Ragobah could never truſt his perſon to his new partiſans, formerly his enemies and betrayers;

betrayers; nor could he rest satisfied by the compromise made with Nanah who by his connexion with Hurry Furkia, the commander of the forces, must have an irresistible sway, he therefore would trust no friend but the Bombay council, who had ever been zealous in his cause; nor would he venture to Poonah without the assistance of an English military force, which to obtain, he must grant their conditions. It was proper that they should have it in their power to act so conspicuous a part and to keep up to it. The reinforcement would give that power, and the very idea of it might already have had some effect in the transactions at Poonah; in such a crisis, to recall the detachment would alarm friends and encourage enemies: upon the whole, if the service of it should not be wanted, nothing would have been lost by its not having marched, and it might be easily recalled; but if once withdrawn, and its aid afterwards should be required, it would be too late to afford it. The expectation of Indostan demanded the prosecution of this measure. On these considerations it was determined the detachment should proceed.

Colonel Leslie's letter of the 20th of May, giving an account of his passage, and the skirmishes he had sustained, occasioned fresh debates in the council. From the opposition of the two chiefs at Culpee it was concluded that the whole march would be thus interrupted, and that, in prudence, the army should proceed no further, at least till the rains were over, as its safety (on which that of Bengal depended) was hazarded by such a march from one side of India to the other in so unfavourable a season, and in the face of an enemy determined to oppose it, who, without ever coming to an engagement, might distress, harrass, and ruin them. It was on the other hand considered that the districts which depended on the chiefs who had committed hostilities, extended but a short distance from Culpee, that one week would bring them to Boondelchund, whose chief was not subject to the Mahratta empire; the route thence was through Bapaul, whose chief, a Patan, though he paid the Chout, owned no dependance on Poonah; that the rest of the way lay through the dominions of Modagee, whose power was great, and friendship certain. As to rains, experience had shewn that the weather being cooled by them

them is more favourable, and besides during that season they would be less exposed to attacks of cavalry. It was determined to write to Colonel Leslie, approving his conduct, warning him to beware of treachery, and not to be induced by any fair appearance to relax in the conduct he had proposed towards the chiefs of the countries he was to pass through; and directing that he should give notice to Mr. Mostyn, the resident at Poonah, of his proceedings, and all such occurences as might require explanation to that Durbar, or the interposition of their authority to prevent future interruptions to his march. At the same time letters were written to the Paishwa, giving a detail of what had happened at the passage of Jumna, declaring a belief that these hostilities were not committed by any authority from him or his ministers, as they could not have arisen from those who were on terms of friendship with the English; that the necessity of self-defence had occasioned the sending the detachment, but the most regular discipline and friendly conduct had been recommended to the commander; and it was requested that such injunctions might be issued to the officers of that government as would in future prevent effectually any thing of the like nature. Mr. Mostyn was apprized of these letters, and directed to act in consequence, and regularly to correspond with Colonel Leslie.

The advice of the order to stopping the march of the detachment, by the Bombay council, was about the same time received from Colonel Leslie and that presidency. The other part of their letter gave an account of the continuation of the uncertainty in the Poonah Durbar, and the imperfect state of Ragobah's affairs there; that General Belcombe had returned to Pondicherry; that the ship Sartine had landed military stores, which were for the service of Hyder Ally; and that the French were deterred from proceeding to Choul by the appearance of the English squadron. These advices were a ground for a motion in the Supreme Council, that the detachment should be recalled to the Bengal side of the Jumna, for to stay in an enemies country exposed the army to dangers productive of hostilities, which might bring on a general war, and if they remained in Boondelchund, that country must be ruined. It was insisted that the principal reason hitherto

therto alledged for this meaſure, which was the effect of French negotiation with the Mahrattas was vaniſhed; for General Belcombe having ſent a ſhip with warlike ſtores to Hyder Ally, who was actually at war with the Mahrattas, how could French intrigue, if it ever had exiſted, have any effect? On the other hand it was argued, that being but thirty or forty koſs from the borders of Owde, the army was equally ſafe and ready either for defence or attack; and that upon conſidering the whole context of that part of the Bombay letter which related to General Belcombe, it was evident that the French were deterred from proceeding to Choul, by the appearance of our ſquadron. That Mr. Moſtyn's letter mentioned St. Lubin being ſtill at Poonah, favoured with the ſame countenance, notwithſtanding Mr. Moſtyn's remonſtrance. It was therefore plain that the ſame cauſe exiſted, and there was the ſame danger from its conſequence. On theſe reaſons Colonel Leſlie's intention of moving to the Betwah river for his encampment was approved, and he was prohibited from moving further until he ſhould receive orders to that effect. The council directed the officer commanding at Culpee to retain the poſſeſſion of it until further orders.

Terms of agreement having been finally adjuſted between Colonel Leſlie, and the two chiefs, orders were given for the march of the firſt diviſion, conſiſting of the firſt, fourth, and ſeventh battalions of ſepoys, who ſet out at two o'clock in the morning, on the 2d of June, from Culpee. For the firſt five miles the march was much impeded by the narrowneſs of the road, and the very uneven broken ground of the country, the face of which exhibited a moſt ſingular appearance, being thickly interſperſed with hillocks of conckar, in which neither ſhrub, or blade of graſs was to be ſeen. In the language of the country conckar literally tranſlated means cinder. The matter of which theſe hillocks were compoſed, ſeemed rather of that kind which we term ſcoria, ſomething like what is thrown out of furnaces in which iron ore is ſmelted; the difficulties ariſing from the nature of ground, were increaſed by the extreme heat of the weather, and a want of water. At ſeven in the morning they came to a well, which was unfortunately filled up; at nine, two villages a little way to the right and left on the

the line of march, gave hopes of relief, but the quantity that could be got from thence was ſo ſmall, and the eagerneſs of the troops ſo great, that it proved of little benefit. At a quarter after eleven they at length reached the village of Murgong, where they found a ſupply from ſeven or eight wells, which had not been filled up. The diſtance from Culpee to that place was not more than ſixteen miles. It is to be feared that theſe difficulties proceeded from want of attention, and not having taken even common precautions to prevent them. Fortunately this error did not prove ſo fatal as it was at firſt feared; only twenty ſepoys, and about as many of the followers of the army, ſunk under the fatigue; a number of European officers ſickened, but all recovered, Captain Crawford excepted, who commanded the fourth battalion of ſepoys, whoſe loſs was great, and univerſally lamented.

On the 5th of June Colonel Leſlie received letters from Bombay, countermanding the orders before given by them for the halt of the detachment, theſe were dated the 4th of May; in conſequence he reſumed his march after a few days reſt.

The notice of this countermand was announced at Calcutta at the ſame time that the relation of the march from Culpee was received from the army; this had been preceded by private letters, which repreſented the evils attending it, beyond the reality; theſe gave a gloom to the appearance of things, which was heightened to deſpondency by the news of the misfortune of the Britiſh arms at Saratoga; a propoſal was made in council to recall the detachment, but it was not preſſed, and the meaſure continued. A caution was given to Colonel Leſlie to avoid the route through Malva, where lay the country of Sindia, whoſe ſincerity there was room to doubt of, and to proceed directly through Berar, unleſs Modagee ſhould refuſe, which was moſt unlikely; on the contrary, there was reaſon even to certainty to rely on a friendly reception from him, and beſides in in caſe of a neceſſity of recalling the detachment, they would, in that country be within the reach of orders. Soon after, upon the news of war commenced with France, orders were ſent not to paſs beyond that province till further inſtructions ſhould be received from the Supreme Council.

On

On the 8th of June the first division of the detachment marched to Jetalpoor, where the whole joined on the 15th. This is a well-built town, it is situated on the south-west bank of the Betwah Nullah, a pleasing river, whose water, perfectly clear, runs over a bed of gravel, the depth about two feet only, though the banks are remarkably high. It takes its rise from a lake called Saugree, and after a course of about one hundred and sixty miles, empties itself into the Jumna, near Bibbipour; the country through which the army passed, was open, and the roads good, but no trees were seen in it. On the 16th, the whole army marched towards Chatterpoore.

Notwithstanding the agreement entered into between Colonel Leslie and the two chiefs, before the march from Culpee, he had cause to suspect duplicity; a backwardness to fulfill the terms appeared in their whole conduct, and subsequent events shewed that the offers made by Ballagee were meant to deceive. The principal Rajah of Boondelchund was Amroud Sing, who was of the age of fifteen, and had upon the death of his father, about six years before, been by the

the contrivance of the miniſters of that prince advanced to the ſucceſſion which they wreſted from his elder brother Sunret Sing, as well as all the treaſure. This junto now governed that country, with them Ballagee had great intereſt, and he exerted all his influence to the prejudice of the Engliſh, repreſenting them as attached to Sunret, and having a deſign to place him in the Rajaſhip. Sunret had not lain quiet; he had a conſiderable number of men in his ſervice, and had made ſeveral efforts to recover his right, which to that time had been unſucceſsful.

On the 22d, the detachment had advanced to Rheat, twenty-four miles diſtant from Jetalpoor. Though Colonel Leſlie had not met with any obſtruction, his ſuſpicion of the intentions of the Boondelchund chiefs obliged him to move with great caution, beſides which the intenſeneſs of the heat occaſioned ſome ſlowneſs. About the 20th of June, on the eaſt ſide of the Belah, the thermometer roſe to 102 degrees, and on the weſt ſide to 107 and a half: and from the middle of May it was not ever lower than 88 degrees. This made the nights very diſgreeable, agreeable, as the ufual remedy of wetting the outfide of the tent could not at that time be ufed *.

Colonel Leflie had now received letters from Mr. Moftyn, who then was at Poonah, inclofing paffports, and orders for affiftance from Holcar and Sindia in his march through their refpective territories; but he had alfo received advices of a force being collected between Chatterpoore and Poonah on the banks of the river Cane, where they had taken poft under the command of their feveral chiefs Ballagee, Amroud Sing, and others, but with what intention was not known.

The troops moved from Rheat on the 24th, and the 27th reached Seerenagur, forty-four miles diftant, a well-built fort of ftone, fituated on a commanding height. They made halt here till the 1ft of July, when they moved to Mulherra fix miles from

* Thefe heats are during the reign of the land winds. A diminution of them is obtained by keeping the outfide of the tent continually wet. Liquors are cooled by wrapping a wet napkin round the bottle; and hanging it in the wind: it is remarkable that when the cooling winds blow this method hath not the fame effect.

Chatter-

Chatterpoore. Here a meſſenger came from Amroud Sing with offers to ſupply proviſions, if the detachment would take the route he ſhould direct, which was towards the ſame parts of the country as had been recommended by Ballagee, and he concluded by ſaying, they muſt not paſs through Chatterpoore. The troops halted one day, to give time for an anſwer to this meſſage, which conſiſted in repeated declarations of peaceable intentions, and of the attention that ſhould be had to the ſafety and protection of the inhabitants, but that the troops could march by no other road than Chatterpoore.

On the 3d the army marched to Chatterpoore, and encamped ſouthward of the town, between two hills, having that town in the rear, the town of Mow three coſs to the weſtward, and Rajah Gur about ſeven to the eaſtward. The place was found abandoned by all but very few inhabitants, ſome of whom were merchants. Three heavy contributions had been laid, and partly collected from the people, for the purpoſe of oppoſing the march; and that the Engliſh ſhould not procure any aid there, ſeveral of the richeſt merchants had been ſent in irons

to

to Rajah Gur, and all were ordered to quit the place on pain of the moſt ſevere military execution.

This hoſtile appearance confirmed the intelligence Colonel Leſlie received of the diſpoſition of the troops in that diſtrict under their ſeveral leaders; a party of 700 cavalry, 2000 infantry, with nine pieces of artillery were poſted at Mow, under the command of Hamet Cawn, who was joined by Gudd Sing with his force, and was with the utmoſt diligence repairing and adding to the fortifications of that place; on the road to Rajah Gur, about ſix miles on this ſide, they had an advanced guard, and had made a fence acroſs the road for their ſecurity; theſe were ſupported by a party of a thouſand horſe, and as many foot, poſted near the fort of Rajah Gur on the weſt ſide of it, under the command of three chiefs; between Rajah Gur and the river Cane Ballagee was ſtationed with another body of cavalry and infantry; and on the other ſide of the river, at the bottom of the hills oppoſite to a paſs four miles from the river, and ſix from Pennah, Rajah Amroud Sing had taken poſt with 500 cavalry, 4000 infantry, and twenty

twenty pieces of cannon; orders had been ſent to the villages round, forbidding the inhabitants to ſupply the convoy with proviſions on pain of death; the few remaining merchants were ordered to ſell off their effects, and remit the money to the Rajah, and then to leave the town immediately. In this ſituation, on the fourth of July, anſwers were received from Ballagee and Amroud Sing; that from Amroud plainly appeared dictated by the former, and meant only to gain time and amuſe till every thing was ready for an effectual oppoſition: as for his own it threw off the maſk; in a ſtile of contempt and indifference, he wrote that the detachment might march what road it pleaſed; at the ſame time he declared to his officers, that he had written ſo, but that he would die on the ſpot rather than ſuffer it to paſs by Sagur, which was the only road now left, unleſs they retreated and took the route by Janſy, which would have favoured the deſigns of the two Rajahs, and for that purpoſe had been recommended by Amroud in the laſt letter ſent by him.

At this juncture two Rajahs of Boondelchund, Gomman Sing and Comman Sing, ſent

ſent their Vaqueels to Colonel Leſlie: they had formerly been diſpoſſeſſed of ſome of their territory by the family of Gudd Sing. Ballagee had ſummoned them to meet him, in conſideration of which he promiſed a reſtoration of this territory, but being tardy in the execution of this promiſe, they withheld their aid, and now ſolicited alliance to gain the Engliſh protection, offering plenty of grain which the villages around abounded with, and deſired ſafeguard: Rajah Sunret Sing brother of Amroud made the like offers of ſupplying proviſions, and with the ſame requeſt of ſafeguards; and this chief's Vaqueel having preſſed that his maſter ſhould join the Engliſh army, Colonel Leſlie, that he might by that means not only have an increaſe of aſſiſtance, but to ſecure Gomman and Comman Sing who were very much attached to him, wrote to him deſiring him to join, and ſafeguards were ſent to ſeveral villages belonging to thoſe Rajahs; but they were immediately driven away by a party from the garriſon of Mow, who, not contented with this inſult, drove off three hundred bullocks loaded with grain for the camp, ſome of the baggage camels, and wounded many of the ſervants and followers of of the army. The Candaharian cavalry were immediately detached, and came up in time to reſcue the greateſt part of the plunder taken.

It was now plain why Ballagee had recommended the march through Mow, and that the ſcheme was laid to purſue every means of annoying the detachment, and that all the moderation hitherto ſhewn was without ſucceſs; notwithſtanding which, and theſe repeated acts of violence, to avoid the imputation of having begun hoſtilities, Colonel Leſlie determined to wait for an anſwer to his laſt repreſentations before he begun to act. But intelligence was now brought to him, that ſome parties had got into his rear, on the road he had marched, with an intention of cutting off his communication with Culpee. This was too ſoon verified, by advices received that Captain Monro, coming up with a ſmall party to join the camp, had been attacked, and after making as gallant a reſiſtance as poſſible, had been grievouſly wounded, moſt of his party killed, all his own, and ſome baggage belonging to the army, plundered and taken. The Candaharian horſe, and four companies of ſepoys,

ſepoys, with a ſurgeon, were immediately detached in hopes of being in time to ſave him, but in vain. He had been left for dead in the field; but a Bramin ſeeing ſome remains of life in him, had given him refuge in a little fort near the place of action, where he remained for two days; at the end of which ſome of theſe barbarians returned, forced him from the Bramin, and in cold blood butchered him in an adjoining wood. His ſervant, who had eſcaped, brought this melancholy account of his maſter's fate to this detachment which he met on the road, and which now returned to camp. While they related this cataſtrophe, advice was brought that a party from Mow had driven off all the cattle for carriage belonging to the army that were grazing at ſome diſtance. The picquets of the line, and all the cavalry, were ſent in purſuit; they ſoon came up with the plunderers, and recovered the cattle.

Colonel Leſlie, finding how unavailing all his repreſentations had proved for redreſs of outrages, determined to repel them by force, and to diſlodge the party under Hamet Cawn from Mow. Colonel Goddard was appointed for this ſervice, with the fifth,

 ſixth,

ſixth, and ſeventh battalion of ſepoys, their artillery, and two twelve pounders. The regiment of cavalry under the command of Captain Aſh marched in the rear, and the Candaharian horſe were divided in front and on the flanks, at half a mile's diſtance, to reconnoitre the country, and prevent the enemy from receiving any intelligence of the party's approach. The road was found much broken up, and worſe than had been reported: this, with a heavy fall of rain, ſomewhat retarded the march, inſomuch that daylight appeared when the troops were yet a mile diſtant from the place.

Lieutenant Colonel Parker, who led the line, directed Lieutenant Lucas to take poſſeſſion of a moſque on the right, which was immediately executed, under the fire of the enemy. From this place they had a full view of the town, which ſtood upon very irregular ground aſcending and deſcending; it was walled round and encompaſſed by a rampart and breaſt-work; in theſe there were breaches, and one particularly through which ran the road. The rampart was commanded by high ground behind, being within reach of muſketry: on theſe hills the enemy had poſted

posted troops, and on a hill opposite the breach, through which the road ran, there was a piece of artillery.

A large tank of water lay on the right of that breach, and extended along the side of the road; this, together with hills on the left, formed the pass which led to the entrance of the town: the difficulty of the approach through this was increased by hills in front.

Colonel Goddard with the advanced guard marched up the road to attack the breach, which he entered under a heavy fire, and particularly from the piece of artillery opposite to it, which was very well served. One of the tumbrils happening to stick in the breach, some of the troops perceiving another opening towards the left, which led to a hill on that side, filed off, and gained the hill after some resistance; the other part of the troops were obliged, by the tumbril sticking yet in the way, to get through the breach by the Indian file *: three companies of the seventh were ordered to attack the heights; the re-

* Man by man singly.

mainder of the troops, as they arrived, forming and ſupporting them; after much difficulty from a ſharp reſiſtance, and the nature of the ground, which often obliged them to crawl on hands and feet, they ſucceeded, having driven off thoſe who were poſted there; by this the acceſs to the town was free.

Before this could be effected, Colonel Goddard had puſhed on to ſecond the attack, by forcing the paſs, where he ſuſtained a very heavy fire, and had his horſe ſhot under him in two places: however he forced his way through the town in purſuit of the flying enemy; he had not advanced five hundred yards, when another range of hills preſented themſelves, on which the enemy appeared with ſome cannon. They were ſoon diſlodged and fled over the plain. The Candaharian cavalry had unluckily loſt their way and were not of any ſervice in the purſuit, which fell to the ſhare of the regiment of cavalry, and would have been more effectual had the others come up. On the ſide of the Engliſh the loſs was inconſiderable, being only about ſix ſepoys killed and nineteen wounded; the enemy ſuffered

ſuffered very conſiderably. Colonel Goddard took poſſeſſion of the place with nine pieces of cannon, with ſome tumbrils, ſtores, and ammunition: the troops behaved with great ſpirit and reſolution. This blow had the moſt fortunate effect. Ballagee, Amroud Sing, and the other chiefs called in all their parties, croſſed the river Cane, and took poſt with their whole force collected on the other ſide, nearly oppoſite to Rajah Gur. By this retreat the country round Chatterpoore remained undiſturbed, and the camp was plentifully ſupplied with proviſions*. Deſer-

* The return of the troops compoſing the detachment, with their ſervants and followers, ſent by Colonel Leſlie from Chatterpoore.

	Commiſ. Officers.	Troops.	Servants and followers.	Total.
Cavalry 1ſt regiment	8	526	1932	2466
Artillery 8th company	10	634	3200	3844
Infantry 6 battalions	70	4964	10876	15910
Head quarters and brigade ſtaff	15		1563	1578
Nabob cavalry		500	1700	2200
With the field engineer			508	508
Grand total	103	6624	19779	26506

The Bazars or markets, with their neceſſary attendants for procuring the ſupplies of proviſions, are not included in this; they are eſtimated at 12,000.

As there hath been no want of proviſion during the whole march, the nature of the country may be judged of from this return, as well as that of an Indian army.

tions, which happened about this time, made an example of ſeverity neceſſary: the execution of one ſepoy only prevented the evil from increaſing. Shortly after the fourth and ſixth battalions of ſepoys demanded in an irregular manner, an increaſe of allowance, on account as they pretended of the high price of proviſions: thoſe who appeared moſt forward were immediately confined; the battalions were ordered under arms, and on the repreſentations of Colonel Goddard, who was ſent to them, all appearance of diſcontent ceaſed; and after making proper ſubmiſſion for the irregularity of their application, they remained perfectly ſatiſfied to wait the deciſion of the Supreme Council, before whom their claims were to be laid. The anſwer from them was a peremptory ſpirited refuſal, which had all the effect that could be deſired, as the demand was never after renewed.

The army had now remained inactive and undiſturbed ſince the 10th of July; during that period nothing material appears to have occurred; the letters from Colonel Leſlie to Calcutta contain only a detail of negotiations with Amroud Sing, begun,

gun, broken off, and renewed, and a mention of ſome obſtructions to his march, from the rains and the ſwelling of the rivers and Nullahs thereby, without any other reaſon given for this delay.

On the 12th of Auguſt, the Rajahs Gommon and Comman Sing, who had ſo early offered their ſervice, withdrew from the camp with their forces during the night, without having given any previous notice of their intentions. This ſudden defection was ſoon found to be owing to the intrigues of Amroud Sing; letters which the elder brother Sunret Sing had intercepted and communicated to Colonel Leſlie diſcovered this: he thereupon determined to march towards Rajah Gur, propoſing there to croſs the river, and force Amroud Sing either to come to an engagement, or retire. Orders were given for the artillery taken at Mow to be deſtroyed, and for the detachment left there to join the army, which was effected on the 14th.

This long halt at Chatterpoore was unaccountable, Colonel Leſlie had been repeatedly warned by the Supreme Council againſt taking part in the quarrels which the princes or chiefs of thoſe countries through which he was to paſs might have in their families, and therefore ought not to have been detained by any propoſal made by Sunret Sing, or other chiefs to obtain his aſſiſtance againſt Amroud Sing: yet this ſeems to have been the only object in his view during that period. The ſuppoſition moſt favourable to him was, that after the unprovoked enmity ſhewn by Amroud it might ſeem politic to encourage the offer of friendſhip of a competitor, which ſtep, by intimidating the Rajah, might change his meaſures, and inſure ſupplies of proviſion. If his motive went further he was guilty of poſitive diſobedience; in this uncertainty the Supreme Council ſuſpended their deciſion upon this part of his conduct, ſo little anſwering their expectations.

On the 15th of Auguſt the army began their march towards Rajah Gur, which they reached on the 17th, the diſtance is about twenty miles from Chatterpoore. Rajah Gur is an antient palace ſurrounded with high walls, handſomely ornamented within and without, ſituated on the ſide of an high hill, two miles from the river Cane, a large town

town ſpreading itſelf on a plain to the ſouth-eaſt of the hill.

Colonel Leſlie, with the quarter-maſter general, and the advanced guard, went to view the ground for an encampment as near as poſſible to the river. Upon their appearance the enemy of the oppoſite ſide began to fire ſmartly from ſix or ſeven pieces of cannon; but without any effect, as the troops were ſoon covered by the advantage of a hollow way. Orders were immediately ſent to bring up two twelve, two ſix pounders, and a howitz: as ſoon as theſe were placed the cannonade was returned, and a few carcaſſes thrown from the howitz ſet fire to the huts, which were ſoon conſumed, and obliged the enemy to remove to a greater diſtance: ground for the encampment was then taken, out of the reach of their artillery. The river Cane is here very rapid, full of rocks, large ſtones, and ſtumps of trees; in the time of the rains it is about ſix hundred yards wide, but a few days of fair weather makes it fordable in ſeveral places.

While Colonel Leſlie was making neceſſary preparations for the paſſage of the river, terms

terms of accommodation as uſual were propoſed by Amroud Sing, a negotiation entered into, and hopes entertained that the diſputes between the two brothers would be ſpeedily and finally adjuſted. But on the 31ſt intelligence was received that a detachment of about 2000 cavalry and infantry, having croſſed the river, under the command of a chief called Puddam Sing, had marched into the rear, with an intention of cutting off the communication with Chatterpoore, which he threatened to plunder, if any thing was ſuffered to paſs through, or was ſent from thence to the Engliſh army, and had ſeized three or four hundred bullocks loaded with grain coming to the camp.

On the 1ſt of September Captain Popham was detached after him with his battalion of ſepoys, their artillery, and the Candaharian cavalry. In the evening he got intelligence of the enemy's ſituation; and early the next morning, leaving the battalion with their artillery to follow with as much expedition as poſſible, he advanced with the grenadiers and cavalry. About noon he came in ſight of the enemy, whom he found drawn up, and prepared to receive him; they had diſ-

poſed

posed of their cavalry on their right, and their left, which was composed of their infantry was covered by a Nullah, and a copse of thick underwood. Captain Popham divided his cavalry on the right and left of his grenadiers, who formed the center, and with whom he advanced briskly on the enemy, receiving their fire, and reserving his until he came close to their line, when it was poured in and repeated with such effect that they broke; they were pursued with great slaughter for some miles by the Candaharian horse. Among the slain twenty-four of the enemy were found on the spot where they received the first volley. The loss on our side was one grenadier killed, four wounded, and of the cavalry, two killed, and four wounded. Some of the enemy retreated to a fort called Gurgunge, which they abandoned in the night; Lieutenant Tisdale was wounded in reconnoitring it. Captain Popham was ordered to remain in that neighbourhood to watch the motions of the enemy, who seemed to be again assembling.

A little before this the possession of Culpee being now no longer thought necessary, it was by order of the Supreme Council given up, up, and the English guard withdrawn: this seemed for a little space to have reconciled Ballagee; but the impediments thrown in the way of the detachment shewed his insincerity, and how little was to be expected from any negotiation with him, or with any of the chiefs under his influence; as Amroud Sing's ministers were so, it was vain to hope that he would conclude any effectual treaty, especially when one of the terms required was a provision for his elder brother, by yielding him a part of his dominion, yet he continually sent messages of accommodation. It was plain the end sought was delay, this was seen through, but the delay must have taken place from the great rain which swelled the river, and made it necessary to provide boats and rafts for the passage, and even then Colonel Leslie thought the rapidity was such, that he waited a day or two longer. He now received letters from the Rajah of Berar Moodagee Boosla, pressing his march to the Nerbuddah, containing the most friendly offers, and informing him that he had sent a person of confidence to meet him on the banks of that river, where he would find every thing prepared for his present occasions, and that future accommodations should be furnished through

through his dominions. In the ſame letter Moodagee expreſſed with warmth the great ſatisfaction he felt in the hopes of ſoon ſeeing Mr. Elliott, who was then on the road to Berar: but unfortunately the public were deprived of his ſervices and abilities at this critical juncture.

He was ſeized on the 4th of September by a bilious fever, and inflammation of the liver, which from the beginning had mortal ſymptoms. The firſt account of his illneſs was written by Mr. Farquhar his ſecretary; this letter was dated on the bank of a Nullah, two coſs to the eaſtward of Serinagur, the 9th of September: from the ſame place a letter of the 13th, gave the melancholy account of his death; theſe advices were received at Calcutta the 5th of October. Something of the character of this excellent man hath been already mentioned: much was expected from his parts and talents cultivated with unremitted diligence before he went to India, but as if the approach to the ſun had brightened the flame of genius, he appeared fit for any undertaking, almoſt immediately after his arrival there. This could not eſcape Mr. Haſtings who cheriſhed and truſted him;

during

during a ſhort reſidency in Europe in the year 1776 his penetration, ſagacity, and diſcretion anſwered fully his friend's expectations, who found the effect of them at his return.

About the ſame time as the letters from Moodagee were received, there came ſome from the Nabob of Bopaul, through whoſe territories the route of the detachment lay in the way to the Nerbuddah: they were in the moſt friendly ſtrain. Advice of theſe letters was ſent by Colonel Leſlie, who at the ſame time mentioned the concluſion of treaties in his own name, and that of the Company with the ſeveral Boondelchund chiefs, the negotiation for which had laſted ſo long; yet he was ſuſpicious of Ballagee through whoſe territory he was to paſs.

The death of Mr. Elliot was of the moſt fatal conſequence, there was not any perſon who could well ſupply his place, he poſſeſſed the entire confidence of the governor general, and was looked on in that light by Moodagee; a few days would have brought him to his court, where every thing might have been ſettled before the arrival of the detachment.

Now

Now a length of time muſt have paſſed before another perſon could be properly inſtructed and reach Berar.

The paſt conduct of Colonel Leſlie, on whom this negociation muſt immediately devolve, did not promiſe great ſucceſs; he had been from the beginning of April to the middle of September performing what might have been done in two weeks, having met but a trifling reſiſtance, and no cauſe of delay appearing, but ſettling diſputes and making treaties in the families of the princes through whoſe country he had paſſed, expreſsly contrary to repeated inſtructions. The governor general was greatly embarraſſed; he propoſed, after much doubt in his own mind, to let matters ſtand for ſome time as they were, without ſubſtituting any perſon in the place of Mr. Elliot, and wait to ſee what courſe Moodagee would take, and whether he would renew his applications: all his letters had ſhewn a deſire, and even impatience, to enter upon the buſineſs Mr. Elliot was charged with; the reaſons which induced him to ſollicit an alliance with the Engliſh ſubſiſted; it was therefore proper at that time to write to Moodagee, only mentioning the misfortune

misfortune which had put a ſtop to their negotiation, and deſiring for the preſent his aſſiſtance for promoting the march of the detachment to its deſtination. This occaſioned a renewal of altercations in the council: the debates in their conſultations extend to whole volumes. This difference of opinion aroſe from the different principles on which the members reaſoned: thoſe adopted in the beginning of the preſent adminiſtration invariably influenced the opinions of one part of it upon every occaſion; peace had been recommended from England as the great object, therefore nothing that could by any means tend to interrupt it was to be admitted: conſequently the ſcheme of extending their alliance to the different ſtates of that region was dangerous; intermeddling in their affairs upon any diſputes, either internal or between one ſtate and another, pernicious; all acts in conſequence, diſobedience to the orders of the Directors; of courſe every meaſure for that purpoſe was to be oppoſed. On the other hand the governor general and Mr. Barwell were of opinion, that to make the Engliſh nation conſiderable, and give its eſtabliſhment ſtability, it was neceſſary to extend its influence; to have

have connections with all the princes of Indostan, which ſhould make them look up to it as the preſerver of their reſpective independence from that power, under whoſe preſſure they had groaned ſo long. This ſyſtem hath already been detailed. From this difference of ſyſtems roſe a difference of opinions upon every political and military matter, not only on the firſt mention of the plan, but on each operation neceſſary in the execution of it. Upon the firſt advices from Bombay of the commotions in the Durbar of Poonah, the ſeconding the deſigns of that council to take advantage of thoſe diſtractions was reprobated by that part of the council; the project of ſending the detachment acroſs the peninſula was called impracticable and fruitleſs, immoderate in expence, and productive of war with every nation in India; the alliance with Berar, a meaſure unneceſſary, and big with miſchief. Nor was the danger from French influence, or the probability of an attack upon Bombay by an expedition from the iſlands, or other arrangements between the Mahrattas and that nation, looked on as real, the conjectures were on the contrary ſide: on the other hand, the governor general grounded his ſentiments and formed his proposed schemes, not only on conjecture, but information which he could depend upon of the reality of the French ministers designs. From such difference of opinion rose perpetual altercations: the present misfortune which suspended the negotiation for an alliance with Moodagee was a ground to suppose an annihilation of the project, and therefore to object to the letter proposed, and to move that the whole scheme should be discontinued. The news received of the depression of Ragobah's party at Poonah, the suspension of action at Bombay, without any communication from them of any future plan, and above all the fatal delay of the detachment having been upwards of four months from their crossing the Jumna to the banks of the Cane, were strong arguments for its recall; for as that distance was not above one hundred and twenty miles, at that rate, in what time was the detachment likely to arrive at Bombay? even exclusive of any check or delay to which it might be exposed from opposition by enemies, it must be a twelvemonth: how then could they be useful against present dangers? Therefore admitting it necessary to strengthen Bombay

against

against an invaſion, it remained to be proved that the detachment, in its intended route, would arrive there in time to anſwer the end propoſed: and it was alledged that a more ſafe method might be purſued by ſending a detachment of General Munro's army from Madras; which might be ſpared, as the fate of Pondicherry muſt by that time be decided, by its being taken, or the deſign given over: and if this muſt be replaced, it might be done by the force in the northern circars; which again, if neceſſary, might be replaced from Bengal; that mode was liable to fewer objections than any other, being ſimple and eaſy in its execution.

To all this it was anſwered, that although the death of Mr. Elliot deprived them of the advantage expected from his abilities and the plenitude of his commiſſion, ſome advantage yet remained; that the powers of the Mahrattas and the Decan were to be counterpoiſed by alliances, which might disjoin the ſtates compoſing them, and unite ſome of them to the Engliſh; that the intereſts of Bengal and Bahar naturally led to ſuch an union; that a ſuſpenſion of that alliance did not annihilate the reaſons on which it was

 originally

originally grounded, or render the march of the detachment unneceſſary: that future events were not to be judged of by paſt errors, and a ſuppoſition that they would be ſuffered to continue: that the march of the detachment might have been made from Culpee to the banks of the Cane in ten days: that whatever ſervice the detachment might act in hereafter, whether for the reſtoration of Ragobah, or in reſiſting a French invaſion, or be recalled at a future period, the preſent continuation of its march was proper: that until the criſis which ſhould determine its ultimate deſtination, its ſituation in Berar was central to all the Engliſh ſettlements; it might be a check to the Poonah government if only meditating, or a defeat to deſigns, if already formed by them. As to the propoſal of ſending troops from Madras, it was liable to yet more objections than had been urged againſt the march from Culpee. True, that in a right line, the diſtance of each of thoſe places from Bombay was nearly the ſame; but the route from Madras muſt be traced along the coaſt to the ſouth, and round the country of Travancore to Anjengo, and from thence, either by a dangerous navigation along the Malabar coaſt, or continued by land

land through the dominions of Hyder Ally; whereas the road from Culpee deviated but a little from the right line, ſo that with ſuperior difficulties the former would exceed it in length almoſt one third, beſides having marches of other troops to replace thoſe ſo detached from the Carnatic.

In conſequence of theſe arguments it was reſolved that Colonel Leſlie ſhould proſecute his march in conjunction with the troops of Moodagee, if he choſe to join the detachment with any, and that he ſhould obey the orders of the preſidency of Bombay for his deſtination; with a diſcretionary power to ſuſpend his march after his arrival in Berar, if Moodagee did not join him with a force, or if he did not receive orders from Bombay: and letters were to be written to that council, informing them of theſe orders, and to deſire that either upon their former plan, if ſubſiſting, or any new for the reſtoration of Ragobah under the conditions before ſtipulated, or the neceſſity of repelling a French invaſion, which ſhould require the progreſs of the detachment, even without the junction of any other power in alliance with them, in any ſuch caſe only to command it to advance. The debates on this subject were further continued, and at last ended in a resolution to recall Colonel Leslie.

This was notified to him in a letter dated the 15th of October, wherein they also disavowed the treaty he had made with the Rajahs of Boondelchund, as made in direct violation of their orders, and he was commanded to deliver over the charge of the detachment to Colonel Goddard, or the officer next in command, and to repair without loss of time to Calcutta, to give an account of his conduct. Letters were also written to Colonel Goddard, inclosing copies of the instructions which had been given to Colonel Leslie, and repeating the several directions which had been given him, as well in relation to his march, and the orders of the Bombay council, as to his transactions with the Rajah of Berar, and a particular injunction to recall any detachment that should have been made from the main body, and to keep the whole together.

Colonel Leslie's death had, before this, put an end to all enquiries; he had at last given orders for the march on the 28th of

September,

September, but on that very day he was seised by a bilious fever, of which he died, the 3d of October. By this event the command had already devolved on Colonel Goddard, a man whose abilities have shewn him equal to any undertaking. He immediately gave notice of Colonel Leslie's death, and his intention to march on with all possible dispatch, as soon as he should, from the papers of the deceased, have got information of the intentions of the board relative to that service, and taken his measures thereon; all which required but very few days.

Agreeably to these promises the detachment marched from Rajah Gur on the 8th, and on the 12th arrived at Goorgunge, a distance of thirty-seven miles, having left the country in perfect peace, and the Boondelchund chiefs professing amity towards each other, and respect and friendship to the English nation, whose power in arms they had felt. The army was plentifully supplied with every necessary for its support and convenience.

Ballagee's territory begins about Goorgunge, from whence the detachment marched on the 14th; on the 16th they arrived at Coutnee Nullah, where they halted two days. Whilst in this camp, a party of vagabonds, professing to be a religious order, well known in the east by the name of Pandarums, about three hundred in number, got into the rear of the English army, and drove off two elephants, and some camels; this was part of a body of two thousand who were in the neighbourhood. Those banditti are the pest of India, roving about the country in great bodies, sometimes begging, but oftner plundering and otherwise distressing the poor inhabitants. Four companies of grenadiers, and a party of cavalry were immediately sent after these pilferers, whom they soon overtook and recovered the plunder, killing about twenty in the pursuit.

On the 18th, the troops moved and reached Heerapour, a march of about five miles only, owing to the difficulties of the road, and of a pass, which the rear guard, baggage, and artillery could not get through until the 19th in the evening.

On

On the 20th, a Vaqueel came from Ballagee with a proposal to Colonel Goddard not to take the intended route by Sagur, representing it would be attended with great loss and inconvenience, as the inhabitants would abandon the city on the approach of the troops, that there was another road as good, and but little out of the way, adding the strongest assurances that if this request was complied with, the detachment should not meet with the least obstruction in its march, but be plentifully supplied with provisions.

Colonel Goddard, satisfied that his compliance was most likely to forward the great object of the present service, which was dispatch, and being well informed that the road proposed was as practicable, and but fourteen miles longer, granted this request, without abating any thing of his usual vigilance and precaution, being ever on his guard against the designs of a man whose character was made up of fraud and deceit.

From the time the army left Rajah Gur, to the 20th of October, the country they had to pass was broken and mountainous and the

roads

roads bad. Every thing now began to wear a better appearance, the country was open, fine, and well-cultivated. The ſickneſs which ever in ſome degree accompanies the rainy ſeaſon was vaniſhed, and all breathed the ſpirit of their general.

On the 21ſt the march was reſumed, and on the 28th the troops arrived at Mallown, a large town belonging to Ballagee, 51 miles diſtant from Heerapour: here they halted until the 1ſt of November, on which day they reached Kimleſſah. This is a large fort and ſtrong citadel belonging to Ballagee, and there it was ſuppoſed he had depoſited all his treaſures which he had brought from Sagur. The fort is ſituated on a hill, the walls are built of hewn ſtone, without any cement; the citadel on the higheſt part of the hill commands the whole; the ramparts of this are very ſtrong, built of ſtone, and laid in mortar. This is the firſt town of note in the province of Malava, the boundaries of which begin ſome miles on the eaſtern ſide of it.

On the 4th of November the detachment arrived at Kourney, diſtant from Kimleſſah twenty-ſeven twenty-ſeven miles. At this village ends the territory properly belonging to Ballagee, and a ſmall diſtrict begins, called the Bilſah Country, belonging to Sindia, but holden for him by a Patan chief.

Hitherto Ballagee ſeemed to have kept to the terms of his laſt agreement; but it was in hope of lulling Colonel Goddard into a degree of ſecurity, which he flattered himſelf he might take advantage; for on the laſt day's march, when the army was nearly out of his confines, he ſuddenly appeared in their rear with a body of 5000 cavalry, and made an attack on the baggage, but without the leaſt effect; a ſtrong rear guard, with the good order and diſpoſition of the troops, prepared againſt all ſurpriſe, left him nothing but the diſgrace of the attempt, and of a repulſe with the loſs of ſome men. This conduct was equally perfidious and unmerited, as the ſtricteſt care had been taken to prevent the troops in their paſſage from doing any damage to his country, which diſcipline was productive of this good effect, that none of the villages in the line of march were forſaken by the inhabitants.

The chief of the Bilſah diſtrict having agreed to the paſſage of the detachment through his country, they marched on the 9th, and arrived at Burſeah, near which his territory ends, on the 15th.

During this laſt march, which was the length of ſixty miles, Ballagee's troops, whoſe numbers were increaſed to near 10000, every day appeared, and ceaſed not harraſſing our rear. At night they retired to ſuch a diſtance as made a ſurpriſe impracticable. They failed in every attempt, nor were they able even to retard the march.

On the 17th the army marched from Burſeah, and entered Bopaul Tollaw, the territory of the Nabob Hyat Mahomet Cawn, a Patan. This country exhibited the good effects of peace, and a wiſe government; the villages are numerous, and inhabited by people who ſeem to live in eaſe and plenty; they are well clothed, and their houſes in good condition.

Iſlam Gurr, or Iſlamabad, which is eighteen miles from Burſeah, is the firſt town of note it is large and populous, and hath a fort

fort built of ſtone. The nabob is rich, having a jaghire, which produces nine lacks a year, and beſides rents from the Mahratta government, which amount to fourteen lacks more.

On the 20th the army reached the capital of this province which bears its name. It is ſituated on the ſide of a hill, and deſcends to a lake whoſe extent is ten miles; the walls of the town are nine miles in circumference; the inhabitants are of a fairer complexion than is uſual in India; their houſes are built of ſtone and moſtly good; every thing ſpeaks happineſs and gentle adminiſtration. Proviſions are abundant; they were much cheaper than they had been found in any part of the march. The force of this chief amounts to 7000 men; he hath a conſiderable artillery, and a great number of firelocks. The fort is commanded by a hill to the eaſtward, which is a hard rock; the upper part of the fort is alſo on a rock, without a ditch; the rampart of hewn ſtone laid in mortar.

It was found neceſſary to halt there a few days to collect proviſions, and make other neceſſary preparations for the march to Huſſ-

nahbad

nahbad Gaut, on the banks of the Nerbuddah. The conduct of the nabob was in every respect perfectly agreeable to his friendly declarations: Ballagee, in revenge for a behaviour so contrary to his views, had entered his dominions and plundered some of his villages; but further outrages were stopped by a spirited message from the nabob, declaring if he did not give over the pursuit and instantly quit the country, he would march against him with all his force.

On the 27th, the detachment resumed its march: the first two days proved tolerably good, and the country fertile and varied; but the third and fourth, on which they reached the Nerbuddah, presented a variety of difficulties, from the number of narrow passes and broken roads, which were such as nothing but incessant labour could have conquered. The whole distance was forty-six miles. Colonel Goddard gives the highest praise to the spirited exertions of his men during this whole march, and the chearfulness with which they went through their uncommon fatigue.

On the 30th they reached Huffnahbad Gaut; the Nerbuddah at this place is not broader than the Jumna at Culpee; the banks not so high; the stream is gentle and clear; a sandy bottom, intermixed with rocks; the hills are very high on the north side, and within a mile and a half of the river. On the south they appear about six miles distant; the ground between on both sides a thick underwood; the river runs E. and N. E. The distance from Rajah Gur to the banks of the Nerbuddah at Huffnahbad is two hundred and eighty-eight miles. Fourteen miles to the southward of the Nerbuddah is the province of Berar.

We shall now return to the operations of the Supreme Council. From the previous knowledge which the governor general had of Colonel Goddard's abilities and discretion, and as it appeared from his letters that he should be in a short time in Berar, he on the 16th of November 1778, proposed in council that the person in whose possession remained the papers of Mr. Elliot, which he had caused to be sealed up on the beginning of his illness, should deliver them to Colonel Goddard, and that he should be directed to carry

carry into execution the inſtructions given to Mr. Elliot, and negotiate and conclude a treaty with the Rajah of Berar, as if they had been originally given to him. This, after ſome oppoſition, was reſolved, and letters in conſequence were written, and at the ſame time the inſtructions communicated to the council of Bombay. Mr. Farquhar who gave the account of Mr. Elliot's death did not long ſurvive his friend; the care of the papers devolved on Mr. Anderſon, who by Moodagee's deſire was gone to him at Nagpoor: during his journey a ſevere illneſs had ſeized this prince, he had been ſome days delirious, and his life ſo far deſpaired of, that he had, according to the cuſtom of the Gentoos, been taken from his cott and ſtretched on the ground, there to expire: when Mr. Anderſon arrived, a favorable criſis had relieved him, but ſuch was the weakneſs which his diſorder left, that his health returned very ſlowly: whilſt he was recovering, he anſwered the letters he had received from Colonel Goddard, announcing the death of Colonel Leſlie, and the preparations making for a ſpeedy march to Berar; a copy of his letter, dated the 23d of November, which was delivered to Mr. Anderſon, that he might

might ſend it to the governor general, was on the 21ſt of December read in conſultation. It began with informing Colonel Goddard that Lalloo Jaddoo Roy, who had been ſent to the Nerbuddah to receive Colonel Leſlie, and after waiting five months in vain expectation of his arrival, had been obliged by ſickneſs to return to Nagpoor, ſhould now advance two or three days journey to meet him and inform him of the ſituation of the armies of the Decan, and all other matters. That the death of Mr. Elliot had ſuſpended all negotiations and ſchemes until the arrival of letters from Calcutta, or of a perſon of confidence to ſupply his place; that as the greateſt friendſhip ſubſiſted between him and the governor general, he could have no objection to the army's croſſing the Nerbuddah and entering his dominions, where every accommodation ſhould be provided; that the warmth of friendſhip not allowing diſſimulation or reſerve, it was incumbent on him to communicate what he had learned, and his ſentiments on every matter; that the delay of five months which Colonel Leſlie had employed in ſettling the affairs of the Boondelchund country was impolitic and prejudicial to the deſign of the expedition; that it furnifhed Ballagee an occafion of accufing him at Poonah, of creating difturbances, and meditating the reduction of that province, thence to proceed in a hoftile manner againft the Paifhwah; whereby the chiefs alarmed raifed troops, and Ballagee received orders from Poonah, and Sindia and Holcar had likewife affembled armies; that the Nizam being in ftrict league with the Paifhwah, had ftationed troops in different paffes and gauts. That he had defigned on the arrival of Mr. Elliot to have with him formed a plan to enfure a free and unmolefted paffage to Bombay; one part whereof was, that both Mr. Elliot and he fhould, in letters to Poonah, affure that government that the detachment was not intended to be hoftile to them, or to meddle in reinftating Ragobah; that it was meant folely to protect the Englifh fettlements againft the French, between whom and Britain war was declared: he then mentioned the fubftance of the governor general's letters to him fince the death of Mr. Elliot, "whereby he was requefted "to inform him of fuch points as he wifhed "for the purpofe of eftablifhing a firm union "and folid friendfhip between them, on the "ground of reciprocal and equal benefit; "that

" that the preſent time furniſhed an opportu- " nity for this, that the detachment would " ſoon enter his dominions, that it was ad- " viſable to ſtrengthen it with a body of his " forces; he waited impatiently to be made " acquainted with his opinion, on which to " form his ultimate reſolutions." On this letter he remarked, that to form ſuch a plan, and eſtabliſh ſuch an union, required time, and a long communication by letters; that the immediate junction of a body of his troops could produce no good effect, but might excite jealouſies in the Paiſhwah and the Nizam, and expoſe his dominions to ravage; he therefore ſhould wait for a reply from Calcutta with the opinion of the governor general, and he deſired the Colonel to adviſe him of whatever plan he ſhould adopt for an unreſerved communication between them, " as ſuch between friends is highly " commendable and approved by God."

In a poſtſcript he mentions the danger there may be from the troops of Sindia and their deſultory manner of fighting, and recommends remaining on the banks of the Nerbuddah till he ſhould receive letters from Calcutta, and to write to the Paiſhwah, declaring peaceable intentions, and that he will not in any manner aſſiſt Ragobah. This, as well as the letter, breaths the ſtrongeſt friendſhip for the governor general. The words are remarkable, " I am induced by friendſhip " to give you this intelligence, for my heart " is pained at the apprehenſion of your ex- " periencing any misfortune, and to return " would leſſen the terror of your arms, and " give diſpleaſure to Mr. Haſtings.

Upon this letter, two queſtions aroſe, 1ſt, Whether it did not appear that Moodagee was diſinclined to join Colonel Goddard, or co-operate in any enterprize againſt the Poonah government. 2d, Whether it did not appear to be the opinion of Moodagee that Colonel Goddard, proceeding on his march, would expoſe the detachment to the greateſt difficulties and dangers.

But theſe queſtions were looked on as premature: for the letters written by Moodagee, upon his hearing of Mr. Elliot's death and received on the 12th of November, contained the moſt preſſing inſtances that the intended negociation ſhould proceed, and might be committed to the charge of Mr. Farquhar; on on the 16th it had been reſolved to charge Colonel Goddard with this negociation, and on the 23d, notice was given of it to Moodagee; now from that prince's writing the letter received on the 12th of November upon his firſt notice of Mr. Elliot's death, to his notice of Colonel Goddard's being ſubſtituted to him, (during which interval alſo happened his ſickneſs) he muſt have been in utter uncertainty; it was therefore proper to await the letters he ſhould ſend after his having learned that change. In conſequence, the queſtions received a negative.

That no precaution tending to enſure the ſucceſs of the detachment ſhould be omitted, as from the delay before Colonel Leſlie's death there might have been ſome diminution of their numbers; two battalions of ſepoys under the command of Major Carnac, an experienced officer, who had a thorough knowledge of that country, were ſent to the weſtern frontier, there to wait the directions of Colonel Goddard, either for a junction with his detachment, for the protection of Nagpoor, or for preſerving the communication with Bengal, as

 ſhould

ſhould be by him judged moſt conducive to the end of the expedition. They ſet out the 4th of January 1779.

In the mean time Colonel Goddard was proceeding; on the 1ſt of December, the firſt and fourth battalion of ſepoys croſſed the Nerbuddah in boats. On the next day, the paſſage of the whole army was effected, a place having been found where the river was fordable. As it was probable the troops might remain ſome time in their encampment, great care was taken to chuſe an healthy ſituation.

Immediately after croſſing the Nerbuddah, Colonel Goddard was met by the confidential perſon whom the Rajah of Berar had promiſed to ſend to him; his converſation, though declarative of the moſt friendly diſpoſition, turned ſingly on the means of reconciling the Poonah Durbar to the march of the detachment: as no mention was made of any further views, ſome other mode of communication was neceſſary: the diſtance from the camp to Nagpore being two hundred miles, was too great for the Colonel to go in perſon, unleſs he were aſſured that the intentions of the

the Rajah were perfectly favorable, in the ſeveral points on which he was empowered to treat; he therefore, that no time ſhould be loſt, ſent Lieutenant Weatherſtone, fully inſtructed in every point relative to thoſe matters: he anſwered the truſt repoſed in him, acquitting himſelf of his commiſſion with great ability. He found that a ſpirit of caution and circumſpection directed the councils of Moodagee, and that he wiſhed all further proceedings ſhould be ſuſpended until a full ſettlement between him and the Supreme Council was completed; that the diſputes in which the Poonah Durbar was involved with Bombay, and the part taken by theſe in favour of Ragobah, was an obſtacle to the commencement of any active operations: at the ſame time there was no doubt but his inclinations to the Engliſh were really friendly, and that political motives, as well from his future views as from the vicinity and ſituation of his dominions, in regard to the Engliſh poſſeſſions, muſt determine him to keep that line. Theſe conſiderations convinced Colonel Goddard that there was not any proſpect of an immediate concluſion of ſuch an alliance as was aimed at in the inſtructions given to Mr.

 Elliot;

Elliot; he therefore determined his course of action by the events of the times.

He had, agreeably to the orders of the Supreme Council, regularly ſent information to Bombay of the progreſs of his march, but had not for ſome time paſt received any letters from them, yet from Moodagee and other quarters intelligence came to him of their intentions to reinſtate Ragobah, and of their preparations for effecting that undertaking: certain of theſe facts, he maturely conſidered the ſubſtance and ſpirit of the inſtructions from the Supreme Council as well to him as the late Mr. Elliot, whence he concluded that marching to Poonah was what was fitteſt to be done on the circumſtances in which he ſtood; he at that moment received letters from the preſidency of Bombay, confirming all theſe advices, and particularly informing him of their treaty with Ragobah, and that their army had taken the field and begun their march to Poonah, towards which place they required him to proceed with all expedition; this confirmed not only the propriety but the neceſſity of the meaſure; whatever might be the reſult of the reſolves of the Supreme Council, the arrival of this

force

force near Poonah muſt be for the intereſt of the ſervice, either to proſecute the war, which he looked on as actually begun by acts of hoſtility he had authentic intelligence of, or bring it to an honourable concluſion, and at the ſame time he ſhould be ready to act in concert with Moodagee in any plan determined between him and the Supreme Council. He therefore formed the reſolution of marching directly; when this was imparted to Moodagee, he repeatedly expreſſed his wiſh that the Colonel ſhould remain in his dominions till orders were received from Calcutta, but nothing could induce him to change a meaſure which he was convinced was eſſential. He ſoon ſatisfied Moodagee that a further delay would prove prejudicial. The whole conduct of this prince beſpoke perfect confidence and friendly intentions. The Colonel finding a difficulty in negotiating his bills on Calcutta, he advanced money upon them, without receiving any thing on the ſcore of diſcount, and in every other reſpect aſſiſted him, promiſing to furniſh proviſions as they advanced, for which purpoſe, a principal perſon belonging to him ſhould remain upon the confines of his country, and forward the ſupplies of grain. All was now in readineſs, and

and on the 16th of January 1779, the troops left their camp on the banks of the Nerbuddah.

In their march on the 21ſt, they paſſed through a conſiderable town called Hurdah, belonging to the Paiſhwa, and here they got into the great road leading to Brampore and Poonah, the way which Colonel Upton had gone when ſent upon his embaſſy to that Durbar.

The next day the army reached Charwah, and halted on account of the extreme illneſs of Lieutenant Colonel Fortman, the field engineer, who died the day after, univerſally regretted. The diſtance from the camp on the banks of the Nerbuddah to Charwah is eighty miles, a country remarkably rich and fertile, and producing a large quantity of wheat. During this march, Colonel Goddard had received intelligence that the army from Bombay was encamped at Boragaut fifty miles from Poonah, waiting there for ſtores, and that a conſiderable force had taken the field to oppoſe them, and was ſtationed between them and that place; and on the 24th he received advices directly from the gentlemen

gentlemen whom the ſelect committee of Bombay had appointed to conduct Ragobah to Poonah, and ſettle the affairs of that government, giving notice of that appointment; this letter was dated the 11th of January, and ſigned by Mr. Carnac; it mentioned, that "within two days the face of "their affairs was ſo changed with reſpect "to the primary cauſe, which led to directing his march towards Zineer, a fort belonging to Morabah, that they muſt "give him advice, if he was joined by a "body of Moodagee's forces, ſufficient to "enable him to advance, notwithſtanding "attacks of cavalry which would hover "round him from all quarters to ſeize his "baggage and proviſions, and if he had "proviſions ſufficient to laſt him until he "reached Broach or Surat, to proceed to ſuch "of thoſe places as he could moſt ſpeedily "arrive at; but if he could not proceed in "the face of ſuch an enemy, without imminent hazard of diſtreſs, then to remain "on the borders of Berar, or where he "could beſt ſecure proviſions till further "directions from the ſelect committee of "Bombay."

This

This letter left him in doubt whether the writers had a profpect of accomplifhing their undertaking without his affiftance, or had given it over as impracticable; the fear expreffed of the Mahratta horfe led him to conclude the latter, and the beginning of their letter the former. This ftate of uncertainty was increafed, by his receiving on the next day a letter from the felect committee at Bombay, dated the 12th, wherein they haftened his march in the road firft pointed out. It was plain the felect committee were ignorant of the circumftance alluded to in the letter of the 11th. In this perplexity he determined to proceed to Brampoor, where more particular knowledge of the fituation of affairs fhould determine the manner of his farther progrefs.

In confequence, the army continued its march from Charwah on the 25th of January; they proceeded without interruption, and on the 30th reached the banks of the Tapti river, oppofite Brampoor, a diftance of feventy-three miles. Colonel Goddard did not find the regular information he expected, but met flying reports of the defeat of the Bombay army.

On

On the 2d of February the following letter, ſigned by Mr. Carnac and Colonel Egerton, dated the 19th of January, from Campoly, was delivered to him:

"Sir, We have addreſſed you on the
"16th a letter containing orders which up-
"on recollection we do not think ourſelves
"authorized to give you, you are therefore
"to pay no regard whatever thereunto,
"We are, &c."

Not having received the letter of the 16th, and the reports he had met foreboding its contents, joined to the ſhortneſs of this, threw him into great perplexity; he thought at firſt of halting, to procure further and more certain intelligence, but not having received it on the 5th, after maturely conſidering his critical ſituation, being in the heart of the Mahratta empire, ſurrounded by enemies, whoſe ſucceſs might leave them at liberty to act with their whole force againſt his detachment, the ſeaſon approaching in which it would be hazardous to keep the field in an inimical country, he determined to march towards Surat with all poſſible expedition. He was confirmed in this by letters from Moodagee,

Moodagee, the contents whereof led him to conclude that the Bombay government had received ſome conſiderable checque, the bad conſequences of which might be prevented by the preſence of the detachment, eſpecially ſhould an attack meditated by the French, be carried into execution. The doubt whether the late misfortune might not operate a change in the favourable diſpoſitions of Moodagee, was another circumſtance impelling him to proceed forward, rather than run the hazard of ſuch a change in returning through Berar; too much time would have been conſumed in waiting to learn his determination, and by that the opportunity of ſervice be loſt. The propriety of this reſolution was evinced by a letter afterward received from Moodagee, wherein he ſeemed greatly apprehenſive of the conſequences of this blow, and adviſed that the detachment ſhould not proceed. In the correſpondence between Colonel Goddard and the Supreme Council, the reaſons which determined him to this meaſure appear at large, and do no leſs honour to his judgment and penetration, than the celerity of his march does credit to his abilities as an officer, and to the uncommon exertion and ſpirit of the troops under his command.

The

The city of Brampore is equal in ſize to Patna, and is the capital of the rich province of Candiſh, under the dominion of the Poonah miniſtry; it is ſurrounded by a ſtone wall in bad repair. The troops during their ſtay in this city were treated by the inhabitants with the greateſt kindneſs and hoſpitality, and plentifully ſupplied with proviſions, which were regularly paid for; the grapes were remarkably fine, and came from a place called Aſhere Gurr, diſtant about fourteen miles N. N. E. of Brampore. Mr. Dow in his third volume calls it Haſſer, or Hazire. It is deſcribed as an impregnable fortreſs, ſituated on the top of a very high hill, appearing ſomewhat like the Table Land at the Cape of Good Hope; the fort on the ſummit ſeems not leſs than an Engliſh mile in diameter; it is of a triangular form, the walls of ſtone, laid in mortar, with round towers, and cavaliers at proper diſtances. Within the fort there is ſaid to be a large lake, and a canal from it which runs the length of the fort; it is alſo reported that this ground produceth grain enough for the ſubſiſtence of the garriſon, which conſiſts of about 1500 men. In conſequence of the ſtrength of this ſituation, the Killadar ſupports his independence, and

and bids defiance to all his neighbours; the country all around is composed of hills of conckar, and such broken irregular ground, that there is no access to the place, but through a deep hollow way, so narrow that a loaded bullock can scarce pass. The mountain itself is of a rocky stone and conckar, and the height such as to be seen distinctly at twenty-five miles distance.

The army marched on the 6th, and on the 9th a Vaqueel belonging to the Paishwah Madharow Narrain, delivered the letter signed by Messrs. Carnac and Egerton, dated the 16th of January, from the camp at Tullingaum, and written in consequence of the late unfortunate convention, directing his return to Bengal, accompanied by one from the Paishwah, corresponding with those directions. The letter of the 19th released him from every obligation to attend to these. From this circumstance, and the further intelligence received at the same time, Colonel Goddard had the fullest proof of the expediency and propriety of the resolution he had taken; he therefore answered the Durbar, that in obedience to the orders of the Supreme Council he was marching to protect Bombay, that his intentions

intentions were friendly to the Mahratta ſtate, and he ſhould continue to preſerve the ſame regard to the friendſhip between the Supreme Council and the Poonah adminiſtration, protecting the ſubjects of the Paiſhwa from violence, and avoiding all hoſtility, unleſs compelled to it by their oppoſition. That he was now advanced to the neighbourhood of Bombay, which according to the orders of the Supreme Council he muſt reach, after which he muſt be guided by its directions. He was then arrived on the banks of the gut Nuddy, near eighty miles from Brampoor, which he had marched in four days: the road was good, the country fine and fertile, full of villages and inhabitants: the diſtance between the laſt mentioned place to Surat, about two hundred miles, which he made no doubt of reaching before the end of the month; nor was he miſtaken, the march was continued with ſuch unremitting celebrity and ſpirit, that the army arrived at Surat on the 25th of February, having marched, from the 6th, near three hundred miles, including two or three days halt.

This march was performed with the more eaſe from the good effects produced by the moderation and ſtrict diſcipline with which this detachment was conducted, which procured them, not only acquieſcence, but every aſſiſtance which the inhabitants of the many villages they paſſed through could give them. None of theſe forſook their houſes, but voluntarily offered their proviſions and grain. An enumeration of theſe villages would yield neither ſatisfaction or uſeful information, and their names are all detailed in a journal lately publiſhed. The country is fertile, populous, and well cultivated, the inhabitants ſeem induſtrious, happy, and humane. Their good reception of the army was the more uſeful at this time as the rapidity of the march was ſuch, that many of the carts, upon which the grain which had been provided at Brampoor was to be carried, were unable to keep up with the army, and had not the country ſupplied proviſions, the progreſs muſt have been retarded from the neceſſity of adapting the motion of the army to that of this part of the baggage.

The firſt notice received at Bengal of the unfortunate iſſue of the enterprize of the Bombay council was from Fort St. George. The preſident ſent copies of letters which the Nabob Mahomet Aly Cawn had received from

from Poonah. From theſe and ſeveral other papers received the ſame day, the whole appeared in the worſt light: for, in ſome of them, it is was added, that Ragobah had actually joined the Mahratta army with five or ſix thouſand horſe, and was united with them to fight againſt the Engliſh.

In this doubt and uncertainty the firſt care of the Supreme Council, after a mature deliberation, was to provide againſt all accidents that might happen from any ſudden irruption into their territory or that of Owde: General Stibbert, then at the head of the army in Bengal, was for that purpoſe ordered to form two camps of the troops under his command, and hold them in readineſs to march at the firſt notice; at the ſame time the governor general adviſed the Nabob of Owde that theſe extraordinary camps were not formed to act againſt any of the powers in the neighbourhood of his dominions. A ſubſequent order was ſent the general to march the firſt brigade toward the banks of the Jumna, there to encamp in ſuch a ſituation as was moſt convenient for defending the Doab againſt an invaſion.

This was all that could be done until more authentic accounts came from Bombay. No very ſudden irruption was yet to be feared from the Mahrattas, and though the defeat of the Bombay army might encourage the neighbouring powers to form alliances with the Poonah Durbar againſt the Engliſh, they could not be brought into action before the Supreme Council ſhould have received ſuch accounts as would have enabled them to take certain and proper arrangements, they therefore ſuſpended their proceedings on that ſubject. The council of Madras appriſed them of their purſuing the ſiege of Mahé, the ſucceſs whereof could not be doubted; this was a ſalutary meaſure, not only as it totally removed the French from Indoſtan, but prevented the effect of diſagreeable impreſſions, which the late defeat might have made, eſpecially if diffidence or timidity appeared to follow it.

Much about the ſame time they received letters from Colonel Goddard, by which he informed them of the ſeveral particulars juſt now related, and the directing of his march towards Poonah in conſequence: one part of his letters was comfortable. They all contained repetitions of his firm belief of the friendly

friendly sentiments of the Rajah of Berar towards the government of Bengal, and of his performing his promises of assistance in every point but that of taking an active part with the English arms. As the Colonel had received no particulars, he could be explicit in nothing but his declaration of proceeding at first to Poonah and afterwards to Surat.

At last, on the 18th March 1779, letters came from the select committee of Bombay, dated the 3d of February, containing a summary account of the whole proceedings, wherein they said, as they could not admit an agreement made in such circumstances, and after so explicit a declaration of the committee's want of power to be of any validity, they should endeavour to treat with the Mahrattas upon another footing.

The Supreme Council had some debate concerning what should be written both to the select committee and Colonel Goddard; at length it was resolved to approve his marching to Surat with all expedition, and as by the resolution of the Bombay council against the convention, or complying with its terms, it was probable they might be engaged in hoſtilities with the Mahrattas, but all was yet dark, he was to act according to his diſcretion in purſuance to their former orders, with this explanation, that as the deſign of his march was to protect Bombay, that muſt be his object; but was to proceed, ſo as not to involve himſelf or the Supreme Council in the reſponſibility of their acts, remembring that he acted under the ſole authority of the Supreme Council, and of courſe was to exercise his own judgment both in the acceptance and execution of any ſervice which they ſhould require him to perform.

The board now, on the 1ſt of April, ordered Major Camac to return to Corumbah in Chutta Nagpore: he had advanced into Berar, where he met with a friendly reception, Colonel Goddard having proceeded ſo far on his way to Surat, it became unneceſſary for Major Camac's detachment to proceed further.

An incident now happened, which though it hath not a neceſſary connexion with the facts here related, yet from the fortunes and high rank of the actor, deſerve a place in hiſtory.

In

In the beginning of February the grandſon of the famous Nizam-al-Mullock, Ghazi-ul-Dien, who, in Dow's hiſtory, appears to have put two emperors to death, Ahmed Shaw, and Allum Geer Sani, the former the ſon of the unfortunate Mahummed, who had the mortification of receiving laws in his capital from Thamas Kouli Khan the Perſian emperor, and the latter the great grandſon of Aurungzebe, and father of the preſent Mogul, came to Surat. His nefarious actions are related in that hiſtory to the year 1761, when every thing was in confuſion, and Dehli in the hands of Abdulla and his Durannies, was a ſcene of blood, devaſtation, and horror. Dow ſums up his character in theſe words: "Thus "ended the public tranſactions of Ghazi-ul-"Dien, who crowded into a few years of "early youth more crimes and abilities than "other conſummate villains have done in a "long life of wickedneſs and treachery. "Though he did not poſſeſs the Decan, "the fruit of his grandfather's uncommon "crimes, he may truly may be ſaid to have "been the genuine heir of the parts and "treaſon of that monſter of iniquity and vil-"lainy." This man, after wandring in diſguiſe through many countries, was brought to the neighbourhood of Surat, where he dwelt in one of the Borah's mosques, in order, as it was given out, to proceed to Hodge: he was in the habit and personated the character of a Faquier: the Nabob of Surat sent and secured his person. He acknowledged himself to be the identical Ghazi de Khan *; he had with him a wife and two children, one sixteen years, and the other nine years old, and about eight or ten attendants; the Nabob sent him to one of his own gardens, called Mahomet a Bang, within the town walls. After his flight from Dehli in the year 1761, he had retired among the Jautes; and wandring from one place to another to seek security, he had come to Eugene the capital of Sindia's dominions. Here, under the habit of a Borah Faquier, he resided a considerable time, and was by the Grand Mullah sent to Surat, thence to go to Hodge, where he was discovered by some of those who had served under him at Delhi. Obnoxious to the Mogul for the murder of his father, and feared as a dangerous rival by the Subah of the Decan: Great sums had been offered for the possession of his person: the Nabob was uneasy, lest

* The addition of de Khan, or ul-Dien is indifferently given to him.

lest when his residence at Surat should be publicly known, his person should be demanded by each of these princes: at the same time it was thought by him and the Bombay council, that the possession of a person so connected with the greatest families and Omrahs in India, might be of service to the Supreme Council. The Bombay select committee gave notice of this in their letter of the 21st of February, and of their determination to remove him to Bombay, which was his design; and they asked the orders of the Supreme Council concerning him. The answer to this expressed a wish that he had not been apprehended, advised that all appearance of violence should be avoided, and therefore recommended to them instantly to grant him his liberty, peremptorily insisting that he quit the English territories, and to forward him on his way to Mecca if an opportunity should offer. He soon after set out for that place, with his family and train.

On the 5th of April 1779 the number of the board of the Supreme Council being complete by the accession of Sir Eyre Coote, they took into consideration measures proper to be pursued in the circumstances which the late transactions had placed the affairs

affairs of the Company in. They appeared to be, that concessions were made by persons having no authority to make them; one of these was the surrender of the Company's possessions dependent on Bombay, and the other the return of the detachment; that the Bombay council were determined not to perform the first; the arrival at Surat had put an end to the second: that it was likely, as the person of Ragobah was now in the possession of the Mahratta chiefs, they would not insist on the rigorous performance of the conditions, so that a peace might be established; but if they should insist on them actual war must then exist, and Colonel Goddard must have been called in for the defence of those settlements: that in case the Mahrattas had taken no instant measures for inforcing the performance of these conditions, it might be supposed they had exacted them either to have a specious subject for present negotiation, or a pretext for renewing the war when they should be in a condition to prosecute it with surer effect; and with this intent might have invited the French to avail themselves, together with them of the present advantage by bringing an armament from Mauritius, where they had force

more

more than ſufficient for ſuch a deſign, the only chance left them of regaining their influence in India; that ſhould this have been done (as ſuch a meſſage, if diſpatched in January would have arrived there in March); if it found every thing in readineſs the force ſent from thence might arrive at the deſtined ſpot by the month of September.

On the other hand, probably the diviſions of the Mahratta ſtate were only ſuſpended by the late danger, which united thoſe parties in one common cauſe; the preſence of Ragobah among them was likely to revive their diſſentions; Sindia, who ever acted on a ſeparate intereſt, might apply the ſanction of his name to encreaſe and confirm his own power. As to the Rajah of Berar, his conduct ſince the knowledge of that event ſhewed he conſidered the defeat as natural, and a proof that Engliſh arms could not withſtand the ſuperiority of numbers, and the rapid movements of the Mahratta cavalry; that his apprehenſion of their power was the ſpring of his advice to Colonel Goddard not to proceed, and the influence of that impreſſion had probably made him give up the thought of the alliance he once courted. It was not

therefore

therefore adviſeable for the Supreme Council to renew any overtures toward it, but if ever circumſtances, either through fear of the Mahratta power, or of any other danger impending on the province of Berar, ſhould prompt him to ſolicit the ſupport of the Engliſh, it would be proper to grant it: the loſs ſuſtained was of credit and reputation only, therefore every ſtep tending to betray a conſciouſneſs of weakneſs or want of reſolution, was carefully to be avoided: at all events, whilſt they ſought peace they ought to be prepared for war.

On theſe conſiderations it was reſolved, 1. To inveſt Colonel Goddard with full power, as miniſter of the Supreme Council, to treat with the Mahratta ſtate for the renewal or confirmation of the treaty of Porounder, provided they receded from their pretenſions under the convention of Worgaum, and engaged never to admit French forces into their dominions, or permit them to have any eſtabliſhment on the Mahratta coaſt; and theſe conditions were to be the alternative of peace or war. That letters in conſequence, and conformable to what ſhould be ſo written to Colonel Goddard, ſhould be ſent

ſent to the Paiſhwa and his miniſters, and alſo to the Rajah of Berar: that other letters ſhould be written to the preſidency of Bombay, adviſing them of Colonel Goddard's inſtructions, deſiring them to be prepared, but to undertake nothing offenſively without poſitive orders from the Supreme Council: and to the preſidency of Fort St. George to inform them of this deſign; and in the event of their ſucceſs againſt Mahé, to order their troops then employed in that expedition to remain there or at Tillichery, and be prepared to move on the receipt of any orders for a junction with the Engliſh forces on that ſide of India. Theſe diſpoſitions were preparations to any plan which it might be neceſſary to concert with other preſidencies in the event of a war with the Mahrattas ſingly, or joined with the French, or any attempt of theſe laſt ſingly upon Bombay.

The firſt care of Colonel Goddard, upon his arrival near Surat, was to chooſe a convenient and healthy ſpot of ground whereon to encamp; ſuch a one he found upon the banks of the river Tapti, two miles above the city. Almoſt upon his arrival he received letters from the ſelect committee at Bombay, requeſting

requesting his presence there. In order that he might lose no time in laying before the Supreme Council the state of affairs at that settlement, he set out for that island as soon as he had regulated every thing relating to the bills to be drawn on Bengal for his subsistence. In this he found difficulties; the merchants, taking advantage of his wants, raised the exchange to a monstrous height, to which he was obliged for some time to submit. The council of Bengal, on their knowledge of this, thought it necessary to send specie from thence, which was attended with a misfortune, five lacks of roupies sent by the Stafford were lost by the wreck of that ship.

Owing to the length of the passage Colonel Goddard did not arrive at Bombay till the 15th of March. The first thing he did was to make them a report of his force, and as they informed him that through the miscarriage of a pacquet from Bengal they had not received a copy of the instructions which had been given to Mr. Elliot, that they might have a thorough knowledge of the whole business, and thereby be prevented from adopting measures counteracting the

views

views of the Supreme Council, he wrote to them amply, inclosing a copy of the instructions, and giving a detail of every matter concerning the views in regard to Moodagee, and his disposition toward the English.

Whilst he was at Bombay he received his credentials from the Supreme Council's appointing him minister at Poonah. The select committee determined to suspend all operations until they should receive an answer from Bengal to their representation of the state of their affairs, with which they had sent Mr. Horsley a member of that council; and as the situation of the affairs at Poonah were very different from what they appeared to be to the Supreme Council, when they sent the first instructions to him, which was on the 5th of February, they having reason at that time to suppose Ragobah had succeeded, Colonel Goddard deferred making known to that Durbar that he had received them, until he should be further instructed on that head. This delay could be productive of no real inconvenience, as the period intervening between the arrival of an answer and the season for action would give sufficient

time

time to follow and complete any meaſures that anſwer ſhould direct: and he prepared to join his army at Surat, that he might be in readineſs for any ſervice neceſſary.

During all this time great diſſentions had prevailed at Poonah; nothing had been done in conſequence of their advantage at Worgaum and Tullingaum, more than what hath been mentioned; the Vaqueels of Nanah and Sindia demanded the execution of what was ſtipulated in the convention, and the ſame anſwers were returned; the want of power in thoſe who ſigned it, the notice the Mahratta chiefs had of that, and of the inability of the Bombay committee to act without the order of the Supreme Council. The arrival of the detachment at Surat had this immediate good effect, that a damp was thrown thereby upon whatever deſigns the Durbar might have formed of recovering by arms what they inſiſted was ceded, and ought to be delivered to them. It had alſo a very material good conſequence in regard to the invaſion deſigned by the French. They had got a very conſiderable force at Mauritius, 5000 European ſoldiers, with proportionable ſtores and artillery, and were collecting ſhips to to tranſport them, and join either Hyder or the Poonah miniſtry; when they heard of the arrival of the detachment at Surat; they ſtopped the embarkation. Thus every thing tended to open a new ſcene of action, with a fair appearance of retrieving paſt errors and misfortunes.

As the ſituation and the different intereſts of the princes of Indoſtan muſt have had a great influence on the proceedings of the Supreme Council, and their orders to Colonel Goddard from the time he was appointed the miniſter of that council in thoſe parts of India, it will be uſeful and perhaps not unentertaining to take a view of them.

The firſt in dignity is the Mogul; he ought to be ſo in importance, but the misfortunes which have attended his whole life, have reduced that prince to ſo low an ebb, that after being at different periods ſometimes oppreſſed and at others ſupported by parties of barbarians who waſted his dominions and abſolutely ruined his capital, (inſomuch that the once ſuperb Dehli is little better than heaps of rubbiſh) his principal ſubſiſtence ariſes from the revenue of a part of the

U country

country of Owde, which had been ceded to him on the ſettlement with Sujah Dowlah in the year 1764. Notwithſtanding his ſituation in life was ſuch as required a continual exertion and an unremitting perſonal attention to his affairs, he had abandoned himſelf to pleaſure and indolence, and was totally under the influence of others. His character is very fully drawn by Mr. Dow in his ſecond volume, and the ſeries of his adventures ſince that time ſhews it to be juſt and true. After many various ſcenes between him, and the perſons who ſurrounded him, Nudjuff Cawn one of his Omrahs, hath by his ſucceſſes fixed himſelf in the ſtate of principal miniſter, with the powers of a Vizir, though the Nabob of Owde bears the title. His rivals in the Emperor's favour had not only failed in their ſchemes to diſpoſſeſs him, but had been actually delivered into his hands, whereby he remained ſole and uncontrouled miniſter, diſpoſing at his pleaſure of every thing relating to the throne of the Moguls; he had under his command a conſiderable army, for whoſe maintenance the many jaghires he had grants of did not ſuffice, ſo that with numbers of men he wanted treaſure. Two predatory ſmall Mahratta Chiefs

Chiefs had tried to enter into negotiation with him, to obtain an eſtabliſhment in his ſervice; but he had no treaty or intercourſe with the Mahratta ſtate; on the contrary, the advantages which he and other chiefs in the Mogul's ſervice had taken of the diſtreſſes of the miniſters at Poonah, to ſeize ſome of the Mahratta forts and territory, muſt have made him ſuſpicious of their ill will, and therefore diſinclined to their cauſe; beſides it was his intereſt that the diſſentions ſhould continue, conſequently no act in their favour was to be dreaded from him or the chiefs who had poſſeſſions in thoſe parts of Indoſtan. The princes whoſe friendſhip was moſt important, or enmity dangerous, from their ſituation, as well as inclination or power, were Hyder Ally and the Nizam.

Hyder Ally, though not in declared enmity with the Engliſh, was far from having favourable diſpoſitions towards them; he had, from the time his requiſition for aſſiſtance againſt the Mahratta invaſion had been refuſed, harboured a ſtrong reſentment, and now had entered into negotiations with the French, and in ſeveral inſtances ſhewn a ſtrong inclination to their alliance. The year befor this, when General Belcombe went to Mahé, he ordered his vaſſal the prince of Chericka, to give him poſſeſſion of a fort which commanded the entrance of the river Myhic; he had ſent ſupplies and even money to Mahé before the Engliſh attacked it; he had given the governor of that place permiſſion to hoiſt his colours for his protection; and he was preparing to ſend a fleet with proviſions and ſupplies to the French iſlands, where there had been for ſome time an armament of five or ſix thouſand men, intended to ſail for the Malabar coaſt; yet he was in an actual ſtate of war with Poonah, in which he had had ſucceſs, having twice overthrown the Mahratta army, and taken ſome forts and territory. His intereſt was that their diſſentions ſhould continue, but it was no leſs ſo to prevent the increaſe of power of the Nabob Mahomet Ally, whom he knew to be his foe, and of the Engliſh whoſe greatneſs depreſſed him, and prevented his increaſe of conqueſt: he is by much the moſt formidable prince in India, having a great number of well-diſciplined troops, and a proportionable well-ſerved train of artillery; he entertains many European officers, and of late has had a great acceſſion to that force by the

the number of French who have found means to get to him from the French ſettlements reduced, and other countries fallen into Engliſh poſſeſſion, particularly the Gontour Circar, where Bazalet Jung had five hundred French ſoldiers. The diſturbances in the Mahratta empire leſſening his fears from that quarter, increaſed his attention to theſe permanent objects of his jealouſy, and his army was ready to take advantage of any occaſion which may offer itſelf to employ it in.

The Nizam purſued his accuſtomed ſyſtem of policy, which is to take advantage of the troubles in the countries bordering on his dominions: he had already profited by thoſe in the Mahratta ſtate; the miniſters at Poonah had, to their great loſs, purchaſed the ſmall aſſiſtance he had at different times afforded them, by ceſſions of towns and territory, and payment of great ſums of money; he was at this time particularly inclined to them, not only from the emolument which might ariſe from eſpouſing them, but by being very much diſpleaſed with the government of Madras: they had ſuffered the annual rent ſtipulated to be paid him for the possession of the Circars to run in arrear; and had sent Mr. Holland to his court to apologize for this, to promise more punctuality in future payments, and to solicit his sanction to a treaty carrying on with his brother Bazalet Jung, who held the Gontour Circar during his life, after which it was to be the Company's absolute property for a cession of it. He had already begun to act with success, when he received from them instructions of very different tendency, whereby he was ordered to insist on a release of those arrears, and a cession of this revenue in future: they had besides, without waiting for the Nizam's answer concerning Bazalet Jung, concluded their treaty with him, whereby for a consideration agreed on with them he yielded the actual possession of the Gontour Circar to them, and they had sent troops to take that possession. The council of Madras added an odious step to this, the Circar was let by them to the Nabob Mahomet Ally Cawn. The Nizam already displeased at this treaty, which though not openly injurious to him, as it regarded only Bazalet Jung and the English, yet as it increased their stability

and

and power, was a diminution of his, was exaſperated at this ſtrange requiſition, and complained bitterly to the Supreme Council of the behaviour of the preſidency of Madras in this unjuſt and ill-timed demand; by the ſame letters he inveighed againſt the preſidency of Bombay for aſſiſting Ragobah. Upon the receipt of theſe complaints at Calcutta, orders were ſent to Mr. Holland to act ſolely upon his firſt inſtructions, to make excuſes for that extraordinary ſtep, and to ſoothe him in regard to the tranſaction with Bazalet Jung, and from thenceforth to look on himſelf as the miniſter of the Supreme Council, and act by their direction ſolely. As to the aſſiſtance given to Ragobah, they anſwered his complaint by ſaying, that as the miniſter at Poonah had made war upon the Engliſh, theſe were driven by neceſſity to have recourſe to every inſtrument of defence, but that he might be aſſured it ſhould never be employed to his detriment, and reminded him that in the event of a war they were intitled to his aſſiſtance: he remained then ſeemingly quiet at his capital.

 The

The Nabobs of Surat and Cambay, naturally averſe to the Poonah government, by which they were oppreſſed, muſt ſee that the diminution of its power was likely to free them from that ſevere dependence, and therefore were well inclined to the Engliſh, and wiſhed their ſucceſs.

Futty Sing Guicawar, poſſeſſed of a great part of Guzerat, wiſhed to increaſe thoſe poſſeſſions: originally in league with the miniſters, he had obtained from them large grants of land, which Ragobah when in power had revoked and granted to his brother Govind Row; he had, on the appearance of proſperity to that cauſe, in the year 1775, offered to yield to them a part of territory ſince claimed by the Poonah Durbar in virtue of the treaty of Porounder; nothing had been yet ſettled on that claim, he was ready to turn to whatever ſide might prove of moſt advantage to him; the misfortune at Worgaum kept him from uniting with the Engliſh, whilſt on the other hand the increaſe of force, by the arrival of the detachment under Colonel Goddard, prevented his forming any alliance or entering into engagements with the miniſters.

The

The consequence and power, and the inclinations and sentiments of Moodagee Boosla Rajah of Berar, fully appear in what hath been already related; from the time he became uncontrovertibly possessed of the Rajahship by the death of his brother, he had shewn a strong desire of alliance with the English, whom he looked on as interested in the support of views, which, although suspended by the late events in the West of India, future circumstances might furnish opportunities of reviving and carrying into execution. The establishment of Ragobah in the Paishwaship was an obstacle to them, and therefore he was averse to his success; the hatred of his cause had grown into a hatred of his person; on the whole it was his interest that there should be no end to the disturbances in the Poonah government; the settlement of Ragobah, even in the regency, much more in the Paishwaship, was likely to bring that government into a settled state; he was therefore averse to every step taken in his favour. This, with a dread of invasion, or irruption into his territory by the Nizam, and the army of the Poonah ministers, inclined him, after the success of Nanah and Sindia at Worgaum, and before Colonel

Colonel Goddard had completed his march to Surat, to wiſh the return of the detachment to Bengal: yet he continued his profeſſions of friendſhip to the Engliſh nation. Inſtances have already been related of his aſſiſtance in procuring money when Colonel Goddard was diſtreſſed, and of his hoſpitable treatment during the ſtay of the detachment in his dominions; in truth he had a particular eſteem for the Governor General, with whom he had been long in correſpondence. Upon the misfortune at Worgaum, he had ſent his Dewan to Poonah, who aſſiſted at the councils held for the regulation and ſettlement of that government, and he had for this received a grant of the diſtrict of Gurrah Mundele * as a jaghire for one of his ſons, aſſigned for the payment of a body of troops, his quota towards carrying on the war. But this had no effect, for the miniſters formed a deſign to arreſt the Dewan, which having notice of, he diſappointed by an abrupt departure, and they had ſent orders to the brother of Ballagee to oppoſe the completion of this grant by preventing Moodagee, who on his

* Gurra Maudele in Reynel's map is on the North of the Nerbuddah, Lat. 23° 10′ Eaſt, Long. 81°.

his part was raiſing troops to take poſſeſſion of it. His averſion to Ragobah was ſomewhat diminiſhed by this perfidy of the miniſters. In April the governor general had written to him, in anſwer to a meſſage he had ſent by Benaram Pundit, the confidential perſon, through whom their mutual correſpondence had often before been managed, which ſhewed that he then thought no force could be oppoſed to the ſuperiority of numbers, and rapid movements of the Mahratta cavalry, influenced by which impreſſion he had apparently given up all thoughts of the deſigned alliance; the aim of this letter was to preſerve the friendſhip and good diſpoſition of that ſtate to the Engliſh. It ended by mentioning that all thoughts of the deſign which had been formed were relinquiſhed, but that a laſting remembrance ſhould be had of his kindneſs, and that every ſuitable return ſhould be made whenever any future occaſion of his affairs ſhould demand it. Thus the Supreme Council, totally diſencumbered from any engagement with him, were at liberty to purſue any plan of action which ſhould ſeem expedient, and at the ſame time there ſubſiſted a mutual benevolence which left

left room for any future negotiation the revolution of time might furnish an occasion for.

That which was most in favour of the English cause was the total expulsion of the French from India. The Supreme Council of Bengal had struck the first stroke by possessing Chandernagore; at the same time sending orders to Madras to attack Pondicherry. This place surrendered after a siege, the particulars of which are foreign to the present purpose, this was followed by the capture of Mahé; they were even removed from Surat, the Bombay Council having given orders for this when they took the resolution of effectually espousing Ragobah. By that removal from the coasts of Coromandel, the presidencies of Fort St. George and Bengal were empowered to act with security from that danger, and by spirited and vigorous measures to repair the mischief of the late miscarriage, and keep in awe those powers who might be disposed to take advantage of that misfortune. The presidency of Madras saw this, and properly concluded

that

that proceeding vigorously in the attack of Mahé would remove the disadvantageous impressions it might have given rise to, whereas withdrawing their troops might have been followed by the loss of Tillicherry, and perhaps have induced those powers who were wavering to declare against the English, and give invitations to the French. Success proved the wisdom of these resolutions.

However, the armament at the French islands was to be dreaded, there was no doubt of their design upon Bombay, the loss of the Protee, joined to the arrival of the detachment under Colonel Goddard at Surat, retarded the execution of this design, and probably might have obliged them to alter the destination of the expedition, as by the presençe of so considerable a force, that settlement was perfectly secure, but the design still continued, and it was not to be supposed that it could be given over, especially as their correspondence at Poonah still was carried on, and they were well acquainted with Nanah's sentiments and Hyder Ally's inclinations.

Besides

Besides the powers already mentioned, there are several whose possessions lying northward partly compose, and partly incircle the Mahratta dominions. Some of them retaining the administration of their own domain, yet own a dependence on Poonah; others are independent: the first though incapable of a direct resistance must have the desire common to all Zemindars of taking the advantage of troubles in the state to withhold the payment of their rent or tribute; this, many of them then did, and whilst the distresses of their masters prevented their exertion against them, would continue to do: this withholding in the mean time was extremely prejudicial to the state, already very much drained of public wealth.

But the independent are more dangerous to the Mahratta empire: many of them have asserted this independence at critical times, when distresses either by internal commotions or external enemies have so embarrassed that government, that it hath been unable to reduce them to obedience. They know that when once power is restored, either by settlement of an able man in the Paishwaship, or by the total subversion of all claims against the

the miniſters, their independence muſt be annihilated. They ſubſiſt only by the preſent diſtractions, and therefore are naturally the enemies of that government, and friends to thoſe with whom they are at war. The countries of the moſt conſiderable of theſe princes form a chain from the Jumna to Guzerat; theſe are the Rajah of Gohid, of Jeynagur, of Jowdpoor, of Odeypoor: the firſt whoſe country approaches the neareſt to the poſſeſſions of the Schah, and of the Nabob of Owde has the reputation of valour and ability; he has a great number of forts in his territory which have ſtood reiterated attacks; notwithſtanding the Mahrattas have made frequent attempts to reduce him to ſubjection, he hath hitherto had the good fortune to maintain his independence. Formerly Gowalier was the principal fort, and the capital of his dominions, but after an unfortunate battle fought with them by his father, four or five-and-twenty years ago, in which he loſt his life, this fort was gained by the Mahratta general, and hath ever ſince been in their poſſeſſion. The preſent Rajah was then but nine years old; he feels the importance of this fort, and no doubt muſt be ready to enter into any meaſure which could enable him to regain that poſſeſſion.

The Rajah of Jeynagur is yet a minor; and the weakneſs of a minority is increaſed by conteſts and diſſentions among his ſervants; his territory is very conſiderable, and may afford an army of 40,000 men *.

The Rajah, commonly called Ranna of Odeypoor, is by deſcent the firſt in rank of all the Indoo families; he is very little known, and whether owing to prudence or fortune, has been ſo happy as to have no concern in the recent occurrences of Indoſtan. The antient domains of his family are now poſſeſſed by the Mahrattas. He can bring into the field only about 15,000 men †.

The moſt conſiderable from power and extent of territory is the Rajah of Jowdpoor, his dominion extends from the borders of Jeynagur Eaſt to the frontier of Guzerat, his capital is Meerta, a conſiderable town; the fortreſs and town of Jauloor, or Shaloor, on

* Dow, 2d vol. Decline of the Mogul empire, p. 86.
† Dow, ibid.

on the river Paddar, belong also to him; his territory extends to Aymeer on the north, and Odeypoor on the south. These two last Rajahs are nearly connected by inter-marriages.

Though no immediate connexion with any of these powers except the Rajah of Gohid is probable to be formed, yet, as by their situation in respect of the Mahratta territory, and their interest to have that empire humbled and disabled from vindicating the right they claim to the supreme dominion over them, they may be useful to cause a diversion in case the war is continued, it is not impossible that some alliance, at least temporary, may be formed with them by those who act for the English nation on that side of India.

The merit of Colonel Goddard appeared in so high a light, both in his military and political line, that the Supreme Council gave him a brevet of brigadier general, and confirmed the powers they had already vested in him for treating and concluding with the Mahratta government, leaving him, in case they rejected the terms he had instructions to propoſe, full latitude of action, as he ſhould think moſt adviſeable: and as Sindia, by his behaviour whilſt the Bombay army were at Worgaum, had rights founded on intrinſic benefits, they declared that he ſhould have a full compenſation for any diſappointment he ſhould ſuffer by the denial of the acts of that committee; that negotiation was alſo totally left to him; as to that with Moodagee, if he found it totally at an end, it was not to be renewed without the orders of the Supreme Council.

On the 29th of May, Brigadier General Goddard announced his commiſſion to the Poonah Durbar by letters he wrote to the Paiſhwa and Nanah, mentioning that it was the ſincere wiſh of the Supreme Council to conclude a laſting alliance with that ſtate, and deſiring they would ſend a confidential perſon to him, to whom he ſhould communicate particulars. The diſſentions at Poonah ran high, Nanah endeavouring to regain the ſuperiority he formerly had, and which he had flattered himſelf the confinement of Morabah and Saccaram would have effectually ſecured to him, and Sindia determined to preſerve his power and keep Nanah in total

tal dependence on him; for this he had retained the custody of Ragobah's person, notwithstanding Nanah had made him great offers to have that possession delivered to him, and treated him with the respect due to his rank; having promised him an annual stipend of twelve lacks of roupees, left him a train of artillery of twenty pieces of cannon, and a considerable body of troops; yet this was but an honourable confinement, he was watched with great care. Sensible that this possession was a great advantage against Nanah, and effectually to secure it, Sindia designed to keep him out of the reach of Poonah, and for that purpose proposed that he should be conducted to a place of safety in one of his own provinces north of the Nerbuddah: this Ragobah agreed to, whether he really thought it most for his security or hoped the journey might furnish opportunities of fortune once more favouring him. Accordingly he set out towards Brampoor with his own attendants, and his force, which consisted of 1500 horse and foot, with twenty pieces of cannon; in this journey he was escorted by 4000 horse, under the command of Hurry Bowagee, Sindia's Dewan. Dissatisfaction arose, the allowance was not regularly paid, nor were the troops of Ragobah furniſhed with forage and proviſions; he heard beſides that Sindia had taken off two of his principal Jemindars, and detained ſome of his people who were to be ſent after him; this awaked his ſuſpicion that confinement was to follow, and prompted him to contrive a plan for an eſcape; an opportunity ſoon offered, as their troops croſſed the Nerbuddah, his artillery marching down from the Gaut of Nurwah to the river, paſſed by the Dewan's tent, ſome buſtle happened, in which the Dewan's people fired, on which Ragobah's troops attacked the guard, totally routed them, killing three hundred, and mortally wounding the commander. Ragobah immediately proceeded with what diligence he could towards Surat. From the neighbourhood of Broach he wrote to General Goddard, deſiring his protection. The General was at firſt apprehenſive that receiving him might be an obſtacle to the negociation with Poonah; but conſidering that ſuch a protection might be reconciled to that Durbar upon principles of juſtice and humanity, and that important political advantages might attend the poſſeſſion of his perſon, he granted this aſylum and perſonal ſecurity,

ſecurity, recommending it to him to be careful in preventing any violence from his people upon the ſubjects of the Mahratta ſtate. His conduct in this was approved by the Supreme Council, who directed him to continue this protection ſo long as it ſhould be not forfeited by any act of infidelity, or attempt to defeat the effect of his negotiation.

On the 12th of June Ragobah arrived in the Engliſh camp, accompanied by his adopted ſon Amrut Row, about ſeventeen years old, and Badge Row, a child of four years old, born to him ſince the adoption. The Colonel wrote to the Paiſhwa and Nanah acquainting them with this event, adding, that they might in their negotiation adjuſt whatever was proper concerning him. The Poonah miniſters were enraged at this eſcape, and declared to Sindia they muſt conſider him as reſponſible for that loſs. It had at firſt the effect of making them in appearance more tractable, both Sindia and the miniſters wiſhing to conclude a peace that they might be at liberty to act againſt Hyder Ally, who was ſtill encroaching on them.

The force of the French at the Island was each day more looked on by the Supreme Council as a matter of very great importance; by advices lately received, they had reason to conclude they were intended against Bombay, and they therefore, in the beginning of August, ordered a reinforcement to General Goddard's army, by a detachment from Madras, and as much as could be spared from Mahé, when the works should be demolished; they advised him of this, and their reason for it, recommending particularly the defence of Bombay, as his first object.

The Poonah Durbar had answered General Goddard's letter to the Paishwa, expressing themselves in terms of high friendship towards the English, and promised to send a confidential person to him; they had even expressed their satisfaction at the manner in which care had been taken that their subjects in the Guzerat should receive no damage from Ragobah's troops, and recommended the Paishwa's collectors to the continuation of his protection. The Vaqueel might have arrived towards the end of July, but besides the slowness natural to the political transac-

tions

tions of that Durbar, by which alone if acquiesced in, the time for action must have elapsed, the general had reason to think that the person to be sent was more to act the part of a spy than of a negotiator; he had undoubted intelligence that Nanah was making all possible preparation for war, and soliciting every power in the neighbourhood to join in it against the English; that he had particularly applied to the Nizam, and received answers on that subject; that the French agent at Poonah was also very busy at this time, and that many dispatches had been sent to and received from France. The General therefore looked upon war as more likely than peace, and precautioned himself against every event. What he foresaw happened, the negotiation was protracted; he had intimated to them that a personal interview between him and the ministers might tend to a speedy settlement, but this was not taken up.

The Vaqueel did not arrive in the general's camp till the middle of August; on the 16th they had a conference; a person was sent with him, who seemed to have the conduct of business, though the first personated ambaſſador. They at firſt recurred to the ſtate of affairs between the nations, before the circumſtances of Ragobah obliged him to apply to the Bombay Council for aſſiſtance, but the General fixed them to the treaty of Porounder, which was to be the baſis of any agreement; the others as ſtrongly inſiſted on the convention of Worgaum, and in conſequence, the ſurrender of Salſet. The General on his part mentioned the want of power in Meſſrs. Carnac and Egerton, and the knowledge the Mahratta chiefs had of it, and told them, that unleſs the requiſitions made by the Supreme Council, (which were, the abandoning all claims under that convention, and excluding the French) were agreed to as preliminaries, nothing could be entered on. No mention was made on either ſide of any proviſion to be made for Ragobah; much time was taken up in explications of the different matters which had occaſioned the altercations and mutual complaints of the Bombay Council and the Mahratta miniſters againſt each other before the laſt revolutions at Poonah, but in the end each reverted to his point. Nothing therefore could be ſettled without a further re-

ference

ference to Poonah. One of the Mahratta agents returned there for that purpoſe.

Before the departure of the Vaqueel for Poonah, General Goddard declared to him, that the Supreme Council would never conſent to the reſtraint of the perſon of Ragobah, that he muſt be at liberty to reſide wherever he ſhould chuſe, with a decent allowance from the Mahratta ſtate, and that on theſe conditions he ſhould not be ſuffered in any manner to diſturb it. The return of the Vaqueel, which he had promiſed ſhould be in twenty days, was continually delayed, notwithſtanding repeated aſſurances that he was immediately to leave Poonah; the month of October was thus two-thirds ſpent in vain expectation; at laſt the general told the remaining Vaqueel that the delay uſed, and evaſive anſwers given hitherto, evinced hoſtile intentions in the Poonah Durbar; that notwithſtanding thoſe evident proofs, the Engliſh wiſhed to ſhew their ſincere inclination for peace, and to grant every indulgence conſiſtent with their honour and ſafety; that therefore he would wait fifteen days more, and if at the expiration of that period the abſent Vaqueel did not return, or ſend

send a satisfactory answer to the proposals transmitted by him, he should look upon it as a declaration of war, and act accordingly: he might the more boldly do this, as his army was in excellent order, complete in military stores, the artillery thoroughly repaired, and provided with every requisite for taking the field and immediately entering upon service; at the same time he had reason to be assured that Sindia and Nanah had set a negotiation on foot with the Nizam, Hyder, and even Moodagee, to make a general attack upon the English at their several settlements. The last was not likely to stir, but the others were but too well inclined to act against them.

On the 28th of October the Vaqucel returned with letters from the Paishwa and minister, referring to him for a full declaration of their sentiments, which he in plain terms declared to be, that no peace should be concluded unless, in the first place, Ragobah's person was delivered up, and Salset restored to the Mahratta government. This broke off all further negotiation. As the General had found Sindia's inclinations so strong against the

the English, he had not as yet made him any private overture, left it should be attributed to a consciousness of inferiority, and be received with contempt; the course of operations might afford an occasion which would render it expedient, for as his connexion with the minister was founded on considerations of interest and ambition, a door would open for treating whenever he thought it his political advantage: this was not likely, whilst his situation at Poonah remained as it then was; his power, by means of his army, and his influence over Holcar was so great, that it was impossible for Nanah to shake off the shackles in which he held him; he had been prevailed on to return to Poonah, where his presence was bought by further grants of territory or large sums of money: no advantage could be offered him adequate to those he reaped from that importance; dilatory and uncertain proceedings were therefore his object. Such a state was as pernicious to the English as it was profitable to him: to them every thing concurred to make decision necessary. The army under General Goddard was maintained, at a vast expence, which the territory in the west of India was by no means equal

equal to defray; in truth far otherwise: the exertions made by the Bombay Council had drained their wealth, and they were continually requiring supplies from Bengal: great as the resource there was, it could not suffice for every demand, and much had been sent to Madras as well as Bombay: an actual existing war gave the English a right to seize the enemy's territory, and draw the maintenance of their army from their revenues, of which they were then the protectors. To the expence of the army was added that occasioned by the asylum given to Ragobah; the direction in several letters had enjoined it, the Supreme Council approved it, humanity required it, and policy made it expedient. General Goddard was bound to prevent injuries to the inhabitants, not only by prudence, but his orders, and the promise he had made to the Poonah Durbar, which continued in force till war should actually exist. That Ragobah might be enabled to restrain his troops by paying them, the general had allowed him 50,000 rupees a month; this expence was thought too heavy, and the continuance of it forbidden by the Supreme Council; thus unprovided he must

prey

prey at large upon the country, unless put in possession of some district whose revenues might maintain him, and such a possession might be extended to enable him to discharge some part of the debt he owed the Company.

The rich and fertile province of Guzerat was the most obvious country for such a provision, as well as for a resource, whence to draw subsistance for the army; it lay open and totally incapable of resistance, no French force was yet in that part of India, or could arrive before the conquest was effected; the approaching monsoon prevented opposition from the Mahrattas, and would give an invader time to establish himself in that possession, the greatest part of the country was the property of the Paishwa family; hence the benefit arising from that possession was double, depriving the enemy of as much as it afforded the possessor; the Nawal of Cambay and other Rajahs, inveterate enemies of the Mahratta state, were ready to assist, if effectually protected; thus the country would be easily subdued, and from its being intersected by rivers and open to the sea, as easily defended against the incursions of a predatory enemy:

enemy: by a proper uſe of thoſe advantages, Futty Sing might be neceſſitated to join the Engliſh, and thereby free himſelf from dependence, and ſhare the ſpoil of his former lords; from him ſuccours of money and troops, principally horſe, might be obtained.

Another very important conſideration was the retrieving the honour of the Engliſh arms loſt in the misfortune at Worgaum: this was not barely a feather; from that event the Indian powers had ſhaken off the awe with which the valour and former prowesſ of that nation had impreſſed their mind. This was ſo not only at Poonah, where the Durbar had uſed themſelves to think of the Engliſh with contempt, and conclude that they were fallen into a ſtate of weakneſs which obliged them to ſue for peace, and yield to give up every thing inſiſted on, but the neighbouring princes whom they ſolicited, influenced in like manner, would probably be the more eaſily induced to accede to their invitation; a fortunate blow, the ſplendor of a victory muſt turn the ſcale; fear, that principle prevalent through the eaſt, would inſpire a dread of reſentment if the Engliſh

Engliſh proved ſucceſsful, and therefore make them await the event of the war. The Durbar of Poonah whoſe great reliance was on an attack to be made by the French force ſo often promiſed, finding none was at hand, might reſume their ſchemes of recovering the territory their diſſentions made them loſe, and deſire a peace with the Engliſh that they might be at liberty to revive their claims among their neighbours.

Full of theſe conſiderations, the general proceeded to Bombay to concert with the Select Committee the plan of operations.

Thus ended the year 1779, in the weſt of India; it had produced ſome great events, and been loaded with many diſappointments; the next is big with many more, whether deciſive or no is in the breaſt of Providence.

POST-

POSTSCRIPT.

SINCE the conclusion of the foregoing sheets, private advices have been received of the following facts. The Bombay Council approved, though they would not be responsible for the measures General Goddard proposed, and furnished him all the assistance that was consistent with their safety; they wrote to Colonel Braithwaite to hasten his coming with the troops from Mahé, but as Hyder had stirred up the princes near Tellicherry to acts of hostility, the colonel could not immediately spare his whole force; he sent one company of European infantry, one of artillery, and one battallion of sepoys, but they did not arrive so soon as was expected: from Bombay were sent four companies of European infantry, and two battallions of sepoys, commanded by Colonel Hartley. Thus reinforced, General Goddard, on the 1st of January 1780, marched from his camp near Surat, and crossing the Tappy, took possession of all the territory round Surat and Broach, and proceeded into the Guzerat:

Guzerat: part of this country belongs to the Gwicawar family and is at present possessed by Futty Sing, and the remainder immediately to the Poonah government or Paishwa family: this was a proper foundation for a treaty with Futty Sing, whose situation in regard to the governing party at Poonah hath been already mentioned. On the 19th, the army encamped before the fort of Dubboy, subject to Poonah; the garrison made at first a shew of resistance, firing some shot on the approach; that night a battery was erected which was intended to begin next day; some attempts were made to disturb the work, but upon its being finished, the garrison abandoned the place, in which were found only a few unarmed inhabitants. The revenues of this district amount to two lacks of rupees a year; it was left in charge of a collector and some troops from Broach, and the march was continued towards Broderah, the residence of Futty Sing, which was held by a strong garrison; General Goddard proposed a treaty to him; some days he remained in suspence, but his deliberation ended in concluding an alliance; the conditions of which were, that the Paishwa should be totally excluded from any possession in Guzerat, and the English and Futty Sing engaged mutually to support each other in the possessions they should share between them. Futty Sing was to furnish 3000 horse to General Goddard, and to have Ahmedavad in lieu of his share of the Guzerat south of the Tappy, and he was to be effectually supported in withholding his tribute of twenty-seven lacks till the conclusion of peace, when his interests were to be taken care of. This settled, he accompanied the English army with his horse to Ahmedavad, the capital of Guzerat; this is a large town well fortified. On the 10th of February they encamped before it; it was defended by a great number of troops, part of which were 6000 Arabs, and 2000 cavalry; the batteries were ready the 12th at noon, by the 14th at night several breaches were practicable, and at day-break on the 15th the Europeans and sepoy grenadiers, led by the gallant Colonel Hartley, took it by storm after a vigorous resistance from the brave Arabs, great number of whom fell; the loss of the English in killed and wounded amounted but to one hundred and twenty, but that of the enemy to upwards of 1000. The town according to agreement was given up to Futty Sing, and a

small

ſmall detachment of his and the Engliſh troops left for the guard of it.

The jealouſies at Poonah had not diſcontinued, Nanah had even projected to ſeize the perſons of Holcar and Sindia, but without effect; but they were reunited by the common danger: upon the news of the march of the Engliſh army to Ahmedavad being received at Poonah, a conſiderable force proceeded under Sindia and Holcar to prevent that ſiege, or if begun to force them to raiſe it, but they learned the capture before they had got half way; that ſlackened their pace, yet they continued moving towards the Engliſh; when they reached the environs of Broderah, General Goddard marched to meet them, they retreated as he advanced; in three days he had got ſo near as to occupy in a few hours the camp they had left in the morning; there Sindia and Holcar ſent him back the hoſtages, writing to him, that though authoriſed by the law of nations to put them to death, they would not be guilty of ſuch inhumanity; aſking at the ſame time whether he meant peace or war? the anſwer was, that the war was only againſt Nanah and the enemies of the Engliſh, to which a reply was given by their Vaqueel, that Sindia was an enemy to Nanah and well inclined to the Engliſh; thus a kind of negotiation was ſeemingly offered, whilſt evidently their ſcheme was to harraſs and diſtreſs the Engliſh army by hovering round them, and not leaving it in their power to come to an engagement to keep them in continual alarm, and cut off their proviſions and forage; in this manner to draw out the campaign till the rains ſhould put an end to it, when they would retire and go to the culture of their farms.

General Goddard ſaw the conſequences of this manœuvre, and ſtudied to end it by a deciſive ſtroke: on the 3d of April, about two in the morning, he marched ſilently from his camp with a choſen detachment, conſiſting of four battalions of ſepoy grenadiers, four companies of European infantry, four twelve-pounders, and eight ſix-pounders, and after marching about ſeven miles, at the dawn of day entered their camp; he was ſo provident in every precaution that his march was totally undiſcovered, and regularity and order ſo well preſerved that unperceived he reached the center of their camp, after paſſing through

a body

a body of ſix thouſand men; he then began his attack; great was the confuſion among the enemy, yet they got ſome troops together with which they endeavoured to oppoſe him, but in vain; they fled from their camp into a neighbouring ground, where, without loſs of time, he charged them; after a ſhort reſiſtance that whole army, conſiſting of upwards of 30,000 men, diſperſed totally, leaving him not only maſter of the field, but of that whole country. The loſs on the Engliſh ſide was very inconſiderable, being not more than twenty killed and wounded.

FINIS.